Unit Overview

Prereading Strategies

Catch a Clue

<u>Objectives</u>

Students will

✓ be introduced to key concepts and vocabulary *before* reading

✓ be able to transfer this key strategy to improve test-taking skills

<u>Implementation</u>

Students will use clues and the process of elimination to predict what the nonfiction reading selection will be about. Copy this page on an overhead transparency, and use it for a whole-class activity. Begin by reading aloud each word, and ask students to repeat the words. Read the clues one at a time. Then, discuss with the class what topic(s) could be eliminated and the reasons why. (Note: There will be clues that do not eliminate any topics. The purpose of this is to teach students that although there is information listed, it is not always helpful information.) Cross off a topic when the class decides that it does not fit the clues. If there is more than one topic left after the class discusses all of the clues, this becomes a prediction activity. When this occurs, reread the clues with the class, and discuss which answer would be most appropriate given the clues provided.

Concept Map

<u>Objectives</u>

Students will

✓ access prior knowledge by brainstorming what they already know about the topic

✓ increase familiarity with the science content by hearing others' prior knowledge experiences

✓ revisit the map *after* reading to recall information from the reading selection

<u>Implementation</u>

Copy this page on an overhead transparency, and use it for a whole-class activity. Use a colored pen to write students' prior knowledge on the transparency. After the class reads the story, use a different colored pen to add what students learned.

Word Warm-Up

Which words might you expect to find in a story about **rain forests**?

tropical	understory	layers
medicine	endangered	sleep
shady	ruin	cashew nut
country	emergent	species

Word Warm-Up

Objectives

Students will

✓ be introduced to new vocabulary words

✓ make predictions about the story using thinking and reasoning skills

✓ begin to monitor their own comprehension

Implementation

Students will use the strategy of exclusion brainstorming to identify which words are likely to be in the story and which words are unrelated and should be eliminated from the list. Copy this page on an overhead transparency, and use it for a whole-class activity. Have students make predictions about which of the vocabulary words could be in the story and which words probably would not be in the story. Ask them to give reasons for their predictions. For example, say *Do you think a cashew nut would be in the rain forest?* A student may say *Yes, because they are grown there* or *No, because we buy them at the store.* Circle the word if a student says that it will be in the story, and cross it out if a student says it will not be in the story. Do not correct students' responses. After reading, students can either confirm or disconfirm their own predictions. It is more powerful for students to verify their predictions on their own than to be told the answer before ever reading the story.

Nonfiction Text

Rain Forests

The Story

Objectives

Students will

✓ read high-interest, nonfiction stories

✓ increase science knowledge

✓ increase content area vocabulary

✓ make connections between the science facts and their own experiences

Implementation

Give each student a copy of the story, and display the corresponding Word Warm-Up transparency while you read the story with the class. After the class reads the story, go back to the transparency, and have students discuss their predictions in relation to the new information they learned in the story. Invite students to identify any changes they would make on the transparency and give reasons for their responses. Then, revisit the corresponding Concept Map transparency, and write the new information students have learned.

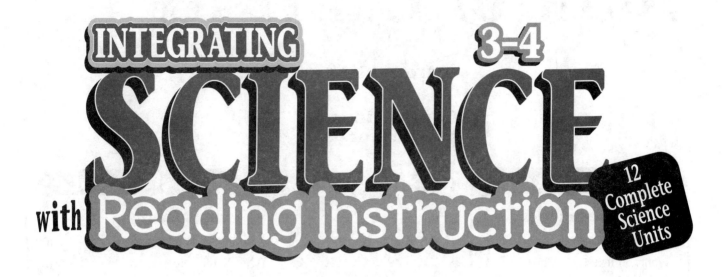

INTEGRATING SCIENCE 3-4 with Reading Instruction

12 Complete Science Units

Written by
Trisha Callella and Marilyn Marks

Editor: LaDawn Walter
Illustrator: Jenny Campbell
Cover Illustrator: Rick Grayson
Designer: Moonhee Pak
Cover Designer: Moonhee Pak
Art Director: Tom Cochrane
Project Director: Carolea Williams

Table of Contents

Life Science

Earth Science

Physical Science

Introduction

For many students, reading comprehension diminishes when they read nonfiction text. Students often have difficulty understanding scientific vocabulary, making inferences, and grasping scientific concepts. With so much curriculum to cover each day, science is sometimes put on the back burner when it comes to academic priorities. *Integrating Science with Reading Instruction 3–4* provides the perfect integration of science content with specific reading instruction to help students improve their comprehension of nonfiction text and maximize every minute of your teaching day.

This resource includes twelve units that cover three areas of science—life, earth, and physical. The units are based on the most common science topics taught in grades 3–4 in accordance with the National Science Education Standards:

Life Science	**Earth Science**	**Physical Science**
Ocean Communities	Earthquakes	Sound Energy
Our Skeleton	Volcanoes	Light Energy
Food Chains	Water Pollution	Acid Rain
Rain Forests	Our Solar System	Electricity

Each unit includes powerful prereading strategies, such as predicting what the story will be about, accessing prior knowledge, and brainstorming about vocabulary that may be included in the reading selection. Following the prereading exercises is a nonfiction reading selection written on a grade 3–4 reading level. Each reading selection is followed by essential postreading activities such as comprehension questions on multiple taxonomy levels, skill reviews, and a critical thinking exercise. Each unit also includes a hands-on science experiment that follows the scientific method. The descriptions on pages 5–8 include the objectives and implementation strategies for each unit component.

Before, during, and after reading the story, students are exposed to the same reading strategies you typically reinforce during your language arts instruction block. This powerful duo gives you the opportunity to teach both reading and science simultaneously. Using the activities in this resource, students will continue *learning to read* while *reading to learn*. They will become more successful readers while gaining new science knowledge and experiences.

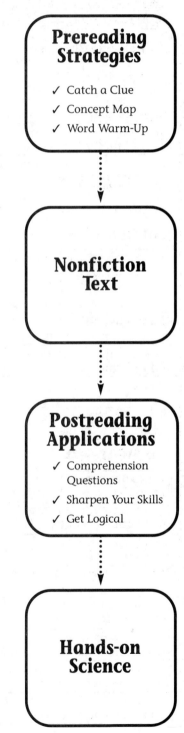

Prereading Strategies
- ✓ Catch a Clue
- ✓ Concept Map
- ✓ Word Warm-Up

Nonfiction Text

Postreading Applications
- ✓ Comprehension Questions
- ✓ Sharpen Your Skills
- ✓ Get Logical

Hands-on Science

Connections to Standards

This chart shows the National Science Education Standards that are covered in each unit.

LIFE SCIENCE	Ocean Communities	Our Skeleton	Food Chains	Rain Forests
Organisms have basic needs.	●	●	●	●
The world has many different environments.	●		●	●
Distinct environments support life of different organisms.	●	●	●	●
Organisms can only survive where their needs are met.	●			
Each plant or animal has different structures that serve different functions.		●	●	●
All animals depend on plants. Some animals eat plants and some eat animals that eat plants.			●	
An organism's patterns of behavior are related to the nature of that organism's environment.	●		●	●
All organisms cause changes in the environment where they live.	●		●	
Humans depend on their natural and constructed environments.			●	

EARTH SCIENCE	Earth-quakes	Volcanoes	Water Pollution	Our Solar System
Earth materials are solid rocks and soils, water, and the gases of the atmosphere.	●	●	●	●
Earth materials have different physical and chemical properties.	●	●		●
Earth materials provide many resources humans use.			●	
Objects in the sky all have properties, locations, and movements that can be observed and described.				●
The surface of the earth changes.	●	●		
Objects in the sky have patterns of movement.				●

PHYSICAL SCIENCE	Sound Energy	Light Energy	Acid Rain	Electricity
Objects are made of one or more materials (e.g., wood, metal, paper).			●	
Objects have the ability to react with other substances.			●	
Sound is produced with vibrating objects.	●			
The pitch of a sound can vary by changing the rate of vibration.	●			
Electricity in circuits can produce light, heat, sound, and magnetic effects.				●
Electrical circuits need a complete loop for an electrical current to pass.				●
Light travels in a straight line until it strikes an object.		●		
Light can be reflected, refracted, or absorbed by an object.		●		

Postreading Applications

Comprehension Questions

<u>Objectives</u>

Students will

✓ recall factual information

✓ be challenged to think beyond the story facts to make inferences

✓ connect the story to other reading, their own lives, and the world around them

<u>Implementation</u>

Use these questions to facilitate a class discussion of the story. Choose the number and types of questions that best meet the abilities of your class.

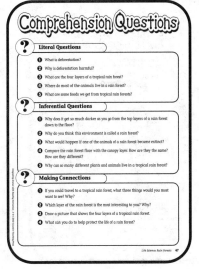

Sharpen Your Skills

<u>Objectives</u>

Students will

✓ practice answering questions in common test-taking formats

✓ integrate language arts skills with science knowledge

<u>Implementation</u>

After the class reads a story, give each student a copy of this page. Ask students to read each question and all of the answer choices for that question before deciding on an answer. Show them how to use their pencil to completely fill in the circle for their answer. Invite students to raise their hand if they have difficulty reading a question and/or the answer choices. Thoroughly explain the types of questions and exactly what is being asked the first few times students use this reproducible.

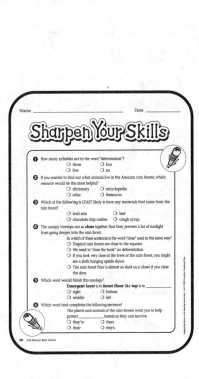

Get Logical

Objectives

Students will

✓ practice logical and strategic thinking skills

✓ practice the skill of process of elimination

✓ transfer the information read by applying it to new situations

Implementation

Give each student a copy of this page. Read the beginning sentences and the clues to familiarize students with the words. Show students step-by-step how to eliminate choices based on the clues given. Have students place an X in a box that represents an impossible choice, thereby narrowing down the options for accurate choices. Once students understand the concept, they can work independently on this reproducible.

Hands-on Science

Science Experiment

Objectives

Students will

✓ participate in hands-on learning experiences

✓ apply the scientific method

✓ expand and reinforce science knowledge

✓ apply new science vocabulary words

Implementation

Each experiment begins with a scientific question. Encourage students to brainstorm answers (hypotheses) and discuss their ideas based on facts they learned from the reading selection. Help students focus on the idea that most relates to the upcoming experiment. (Additional teacher background information and experiment results are provided to enhance discussions.) Review the step-by-step procedure for the hands-on experiment with the class, and provide them with the necessary materials for the activity.

Give each student a copy of the corresponding reproducibles that use the steps of the scientific method. Have students read and follow the directions to complete the experiment. Discuss the questions in the Results and Conclusions section, and have students write their answers on their page. The final question in this section restates the inquiry used to start the activity.

Catch a Clue

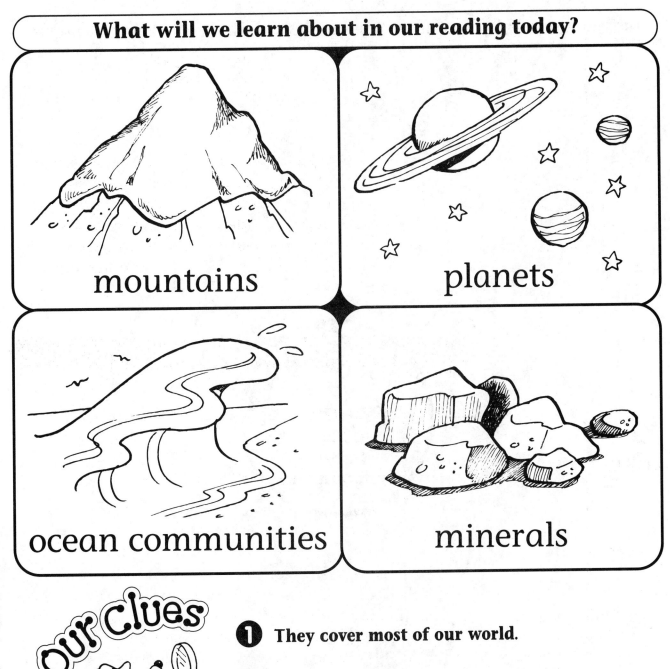

What will we learn about in our reading today?

mountains

planets

ocean communities

minerals

Our Clues

1. They cover most of our world.

2. Many plants and animals live there.

3. They have different communities of life.

4. They need to be protected.

Concept Map

Facts we already know about **ocean communities,** and the new facts we have learned

Ocean Communities

Integrating Science with Reading Instruction · 3–4 © 2002 Creative Teaching Press

Word Warm-Up

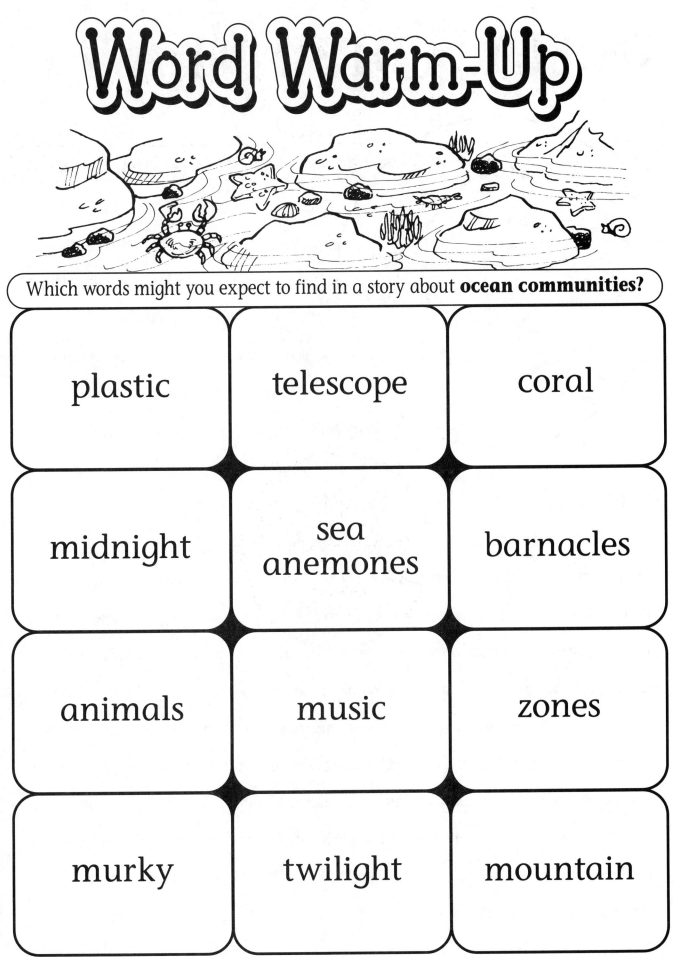

Which words might you expect to find in a story about **ocean communities?**

plastic	telescope	coral
midnight	sea anemones	barnacles
animals	music	zones
murky	twilight	mountain

Ocean Communities

Dear Maria,

I am having a great time with my uncle in California. We went to the beach. I saw the ocean for the first time. When we first got to the beach, my uncle told me there was a low tide. He said that means the waves would not go high up on the beach. I fell asleep lying out in the sun. When I woke up, I felt my feet getting wet! I thought my uncle had played a trick on me. Then, I saw the waves come up high on the beach. My uncle told me this was called a high tide. We had to move our towels to stay dry. It was funny!

Later, we walked along the shore on the sandy beach. I saw clams, mole crabs, worms, sand dollars, and some types of grass. The animals would bury themselves in the sand for part of the day. A little farther along the shore, there was a rocky tide pool. I had never seen a tide pool before. My uncle explained that tide pools are made on a rocky shore area. When the ocean water has a low tide, water is left in pools between the rocks. He also told me that tide pools have different zones where plants and animals live. Sea urchins, sea anemones, and sea stars live in the deepest parts. They cannot live out of the water. The sea urchins and sea stars crawl into a pool of water as the tide is going back out. Hermit crabs, barnacles, and mussels live in the middle area. When the tide goes out, barnacles and mussels close up and store water in their shells. This is how they live until the tide comes back in and covers them with water again. Limpets and chiton live in the high tide zone. They can live out of the water while the tide is out. I saw the coolest sea urchin. I took a picture of it to show you.

Integrating Science with Reading Instruction · 3-4 © 2002 Creative Teaching Press

Last week, my uncle and I went on a guided tour boat. We visited the open ocean. The water is much deeper there. The tour guide knew a lot about the ocean. I learned that the oceans cover three fourths of the earth and they are so big and deep that there are different types of homes in the ocean. The water at the surface of the ocean is called the Sunlight Zone. That means the sun can shine down through the water. This zone is where most of the animals of the ocean live. Below the Sunlight Zone is the Twilight Zone. The tour guide said it is very murky there and hard to see. If you went deeper into the ocean, you would come to the Midnight Zone. It is below the Twilight Zone. It is pitch black and very cold. I do not think I would want to visit down there. Would you?

I sure loved visiting the ocean! I cannot wait to get back so I can show you all of the pictures I took and the cool shells I collected from the beach. My uncle said you could come with us next time. It would be so fun to learn more about the ocean together!

Your best friend,

Jackie

Comprehension Questions

? Literal Questions

1. What is an ocean?

2. What are the different zones in the open ocean?

3. What animals live on a sandy beach?

4. What animals live in a rocky tide pool?

5. What happens when there is a low tide?

? Inferential Questions

1. What are some differences between a tide pool and the open ocean? Be specific.

2. Why do you think the zones of the open ocean are called Sunlight, Twilight, and Midnight?

3. Why do you think most animals live in the Sunlight Zone?

4. Would you be able to jump off of a boat and dive down to the Twilight Zone? Why or why not?

5. What zone(s) do you think submarines travel in?

? Making Connections

1. Have you ever been to the ocean? What did you see or would you expect to see?

2. Which ocean community would you most like to see up close? Why?

3. Imagine that you could spend a day in each ocean community (the beach, a tide pool, and the open ocean) as a living creature. Which creature would you want to be in each environment? Why?

4. Does this story remind you of any books, magazines, Internet sites, or television shows? If so, which ones? Why?

Integrating Science with Reading Instruction · 3–4 © 2002 Creative Teaching Press

Name _____   Date _____

Sharpen Your Skills

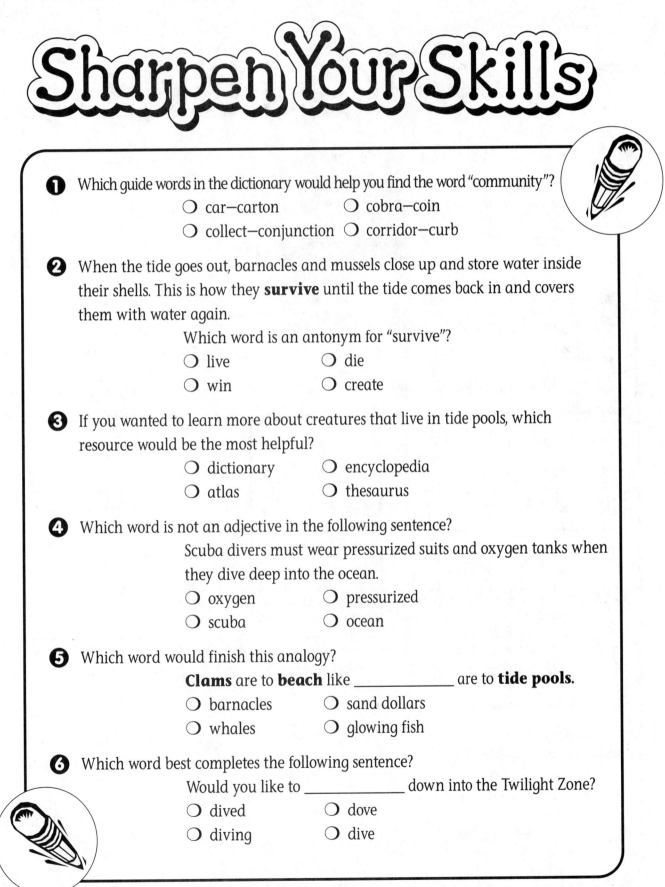

1 Which guide words in the dictionary would help you find the word "community"?

○ car–carton   ○ cobra–coin

○ collect–conjunction   ○ corridor–curb

2 When the tide goes out, barnacles and mussels close up and store water inside their shells. This is how they **survive** until the tide comes back in and covers them with water again.

Which word is an antonym for "survive"?

○ live   ○ die

○ win   ○ create

3 If you wanted to learn more about creatures that live in tide pools, which resource would be the most helpful?

○ dictionary   ○ encyclopedia

○ atlas   ○ thesaurus

4 Which word is not an adjective in the following sentence?

Scuba divers must wear pressurized suits and oxygen tanks when they dive deep into the ocean.

○ oxygen   ○ pressurized

○ scuba   ○ ocean

5 Which word would finish this analogy?

Clams are to **beach** like _____ are to **tide pools**.

○ barnacles   ○ sand dollars

○ whales   ○ glowing fish

6 Which word best completes the following sentence?

Would you like to _____ down into the Twilight Zone?

○ dived   ○ dove

○ diving   ○ dive

Integrating Science with Reading Instruction · 3–4 © 2002 Creative Teaching Press

Name _____   Date _____

Get Logical

Reggie, Shasta, Carmine, and Shirley each read a book over the summer that taught them about the ocean community they were most interested in. Use the clues below to find out which community each person learned more about.

Clues

1 Shasta learned more about mole crabs and sand dollars.

2 Reggie learned more about the cold, pitch black area of the ocean.

3 Shirley's book told her about the rocky shore area when the ocean has low tide.

4 Carmine learned about plants and animals that live in clear, warm, tropical waters.

	Reggie	Shasta	Carmine	Shirley
Tide Pools				
Sandy Beach				
Midnight Zone				
Coral Reef				

Reggie read more about the _____.

Shasta read more about the _____.

Carmine read more about the _____.

Shirley read more about the _____.

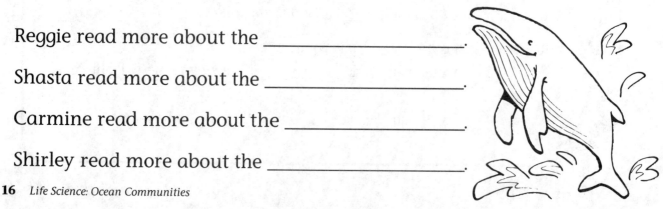

Integrating Science with Reading Instruction · 3–4 © 2002 Creative Teaching Press

Ocean Communities

How do animals survive in a tide pool?

Teacher Background Information

Tide pools form in rocky coastal regions where water is trapped between the rocks as the tide goes out. Tides are mainly the result of the gravitational pull of the moon on the earth with a little help sometimes from the sun. Because the water recedes and returns gradually as the tide is going out and coming in, the animals that live in a tide pool have time to adjust to the changing water level. They are adapted in many ways to being in and out of the water. The animals that live highest up on the rocks must be able to survive out of the water the longest. Many, like the barnacle and periwinkle snail, close up and store water inside their shells to keep them alive. Other animals, like some crabs and sea stars, must migrate into deeper water or find a pool to stay in until the tide returns. Tide pools are very interesting environments to visit when the tide is low, and you can see many of the varied creatures that make this ocean community their home.

Experiment Results

The low spots, or depressions, nearest the ocean will fill with water first as the tide comes in. High tide is represented when the pan is full of water. At this time, all of the animals should be under the water, or almost covered with water. As students remove the water to simulate the tide going out, the snail will be uncovered first, then the sea star, and finally the crab. However, the students should note that in real life the sea star and perhaps the crab are still covered with water, since they would need to migrate to a tide pool. Crabs usually swim into deeper water as the tide goes out. The lowest water level represents low tide. The tides are caused primarily by the gravitational pull of the moon. This community is called a rocky tide pool because it is found along a rocky shore, and the water collects in pools as the tide goes out.

Ocean Communities

How do animals survive in a tide pool?

Procedure

1 Use the modeling clay to build a downward sloping landscape at one end of the pan. Leave about half of the pan empty. (This will be the area for the deeper ocean water.)

2 Use your hand to make several indents (like shallow holes) in the surface of the clay to form places for pools of water to collect.

3 Press rocks and pebbles into the clay, especially around your indents.

4 Place the plastic snail high up on your "shoreline," and place the sea star in the middle of the slope (in one of the indents). Gently press both of them into the clay. Then, place the plastic crab farthest down the slope (near the bottom of the clay).

5 Add three to four drops of blue food coloring to your pitcher of water to create "ocean water."

6 Slowly pour the water into the empty end of the pan. (Do not let the water overflow.) Observe how the "tide" comes in as the water moves up the clay.

7 Use the turkey baster to suck up and remove some of the water from your landscape (clay area). Empty the water from the turkey baster into the pitcher. Keep removing water with the turkey baster until you reach a "low tide." This is where the water is trapped in the indents or "pools" you formed. Observe where the animals are located.

MATERIALS

(per group)
- ✔ modeling clay
- ✔ rectangular disposable aluminum pan
- ✔ rocks and pebbles
- ✔ plastic sea star, crab, and snail
- ✔ blue food coloring
- ✔ pitcher of water
- ✔ turkey baster

Integrating Science with Reading Instruction · 3–4 © 2002 Creative Teaching Press

Name _____   Date _____

Ocean Communities

How do animals survive in a tide pool?

Results and Conclusions

1 Which areas of your "tide pool" filled up with water first as the tide came in?

_____

2 What is the name for the time period when your pan was full of water?

_____

Which animals were underwater during that time period?

_____

3 As you removed water from your tide pool environment, which animal(s) were exposed to the air first?

_____

4 Which animal(s) must move into a pool as the water level gets lower?

_____

5 Which animal might swim into the deeper water as the tide goes out?

_____

6 What do you call the time period when your pan had the lowest water level?

_____

7 Why do you think this ocean community is called a rocky tide pool?

_____

8 How do animals survive in a tide pool?

_____

Integrating Science with Reading Instruction · 3–4 © 2002 Creative Teaching Press

Catch a Clue

What will we learn about in our reading today?

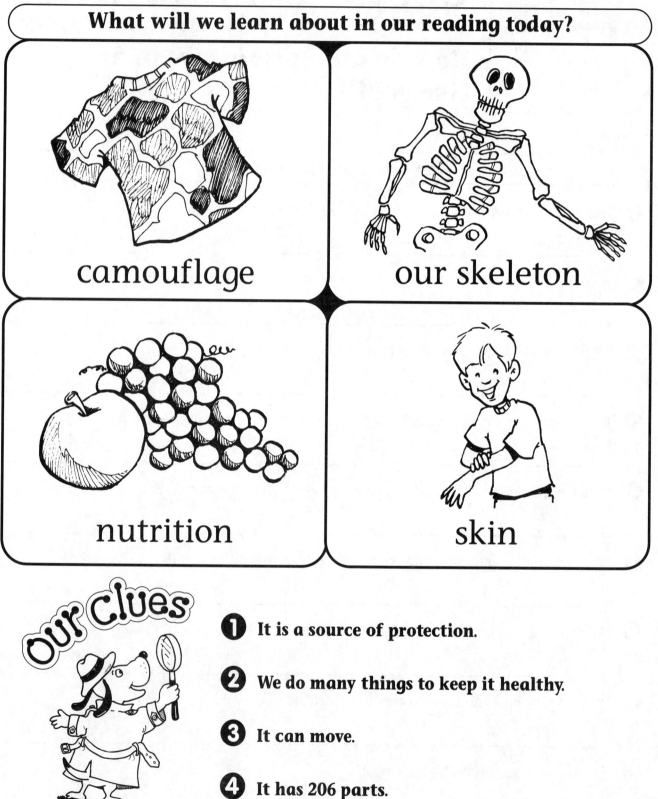

camouflage

our skeleton

nutrition

skin

Our Clues

1 It is a source of protection.

2 We do many things to keep it healthy.

3 It can move.

4 It has 206 parts.

Integrating Science with Reading Instruction · 3–4 © 2002 Creative Teaching Press

Concept Map

Facts we already know about **our skeleton,** and the new facts we have learned

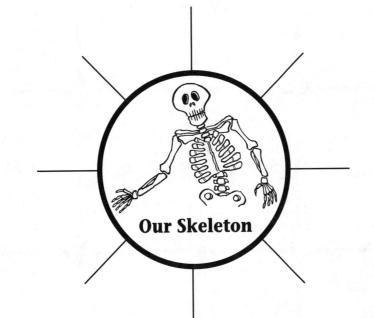

Our Skeleton

Word Warm-Up

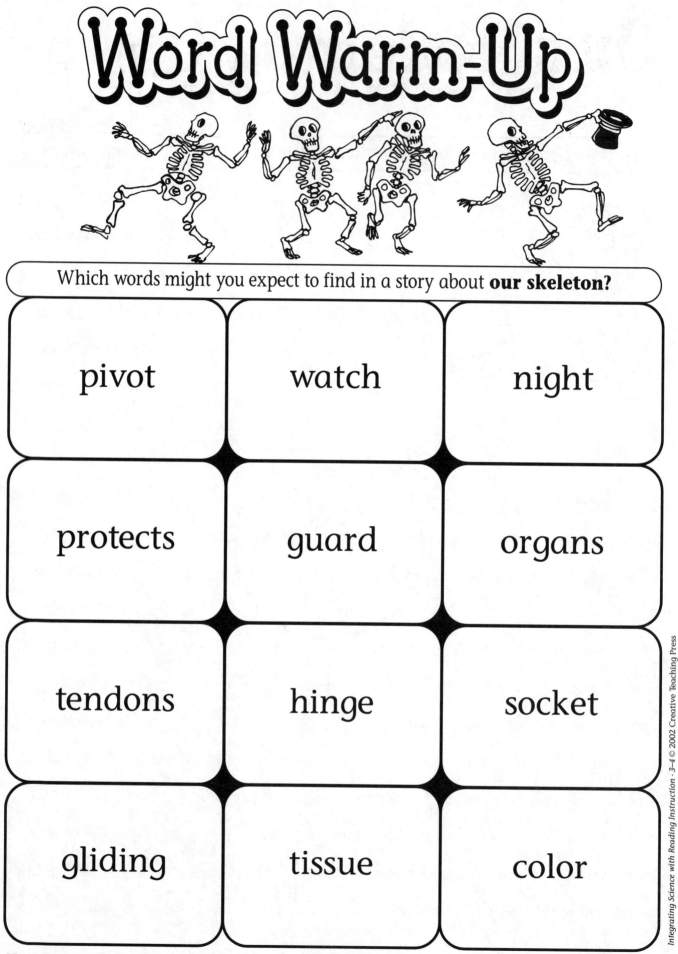

Which words might you expect to find in a story about **our skeleton?**

pivot	watch	night
protects	guard	organs
tendons	hinge	socket
gliding	tissue	color

Integrating Science with Reading Instruction · 3–4 © 2002 Creative Teaching Press

Our Skeleton

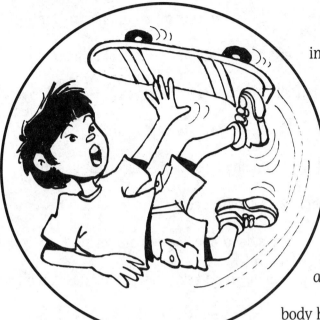

Ouch, what a painful experience! I was skateboarding to school when suddenly my board hit a rock and I fell and hit my arm on the concrete. My arm was hurting so badly that my mom had to rush me to the doctor's office. Boy, I sure learned a lot during that visit. Not only did I find out I had a broken bone, but the doctor explained bones and our skeleton to me. Did you know that your body has 206 bones that help you to stand straight and tall? Lucky for me, I only broke one of my 206 bones.

Bones help you in many ways. They help you move around. Your bones guard the organs that keep you alive. The bones in your arms and legs are long. The bones in your fingers and toes are short. Did you know your hand is made of 26 bones? I am so glad I did not break any of those. Your rib bones guard your heart and lungs and keep you from getting hurt if you fall. Your skull bones guard your brain. You also have bones along your spine called vertebrae. They keep your spinal cord safe. The smallest bone in your body is called the stirrup. It is in your inner ear. You use the longest bone in your body to run. Can you guess what it is? It is your thighbone. It is also called the femur.

The doctor told me I was lucky that I only broke a bone and did not tear any ligaments or tendons. He explained to me that the bones in your body do not work all by themselves. They are connected to other bones in your body by strong stretchy bands called ligaments. He also said muscles are connected to your bones by tough cords called tendons. You can move your skeleton with the help of your muscles. He told me that the places where bones meet each other are called joints.

Integrating Science with Reading Instruction · 3–4 © 2002 Creative Teaching Press

The most interesting thing the doctor told me was that there are six different kinds of joints in your body! Each type allows your bones to move in a different way. Ball-and-socket joints let us move in many directions. Your shoulders and hips have ball-and-socket joints to allow your arms and legs to move up and down, out to the side, and all around. It is the ball-and-socket joints that help us pitch a baseball to a batter. Hinge joints let your bones bend or straighten at the joint. This is just like the hinge on a door or when you bend your elbow. Another type of joint is called a pivot joint. This joint helps to move bones from side to side. Shake your head from side to side like you are saying "no." You just used a pivot joint. Gliding joints help bones move up and down and side to side. You have gliding joints in your neck, wrist, and ankle. They let you nod your head to say "yes" or make a 3-point shot in a basketball game. Another type of joint is called an immovable joint. This joint does not let your bones move at all! This type of joint is found in your skull. The last type of joint is called a partially movable joint. This joint lets you twist and bend in different ways. Where do you think these joints are? If you guessed that they are in your backbone, you are right!

Finally, the doctor told me that the bones in your body are living tissue. That means they grow and need to be taken care of. He said I need calcium, vitamin D, and lots of exercise in order for my bones to be strong and healthy. If people do not get enough of these three things, their bones can actually become weaker. I told the doctor that I drink a lot of milk, eat dairy products and other healthy foods, and gets lots of exercise every day skateboarding to help me grow strong, healthy bones.

Integrating Science with Reading Instruction · 3–4 © 2002 Creative Teaching Press

Comprehension Questions

Integrating Science with Reading Instruction · 3-4 © 2002 Creative Teaching Press

? Literal Questions

1 How many bones are in your body? How many are in your hand?

2 What are ligaments?

3 Which bones keep your spinal cord safe?

4 What are the different kinds of joints that you have in your body?

5 What will happen if you do not take care of your skeleton?

? Inferential Questions

1 Why is it important to have immovable joints in your skull?

2 What kind of joint(s) do you use to kick a ball?

3 What would happen if you did not have bones in your body?

4 Why do you think people have to wear a cast when they break a leg?

5 What joints allow you to roll your head around in a circle?

? Making Connections

1 What should you eat to keep your bones healthy?

2 What activities do you do when you use your ball-and-socket joints?

3 What activities do you do at school and home using your gliding joints?

4 Which bones do you use the most in your favorite activities?

Sharpen Your Skills

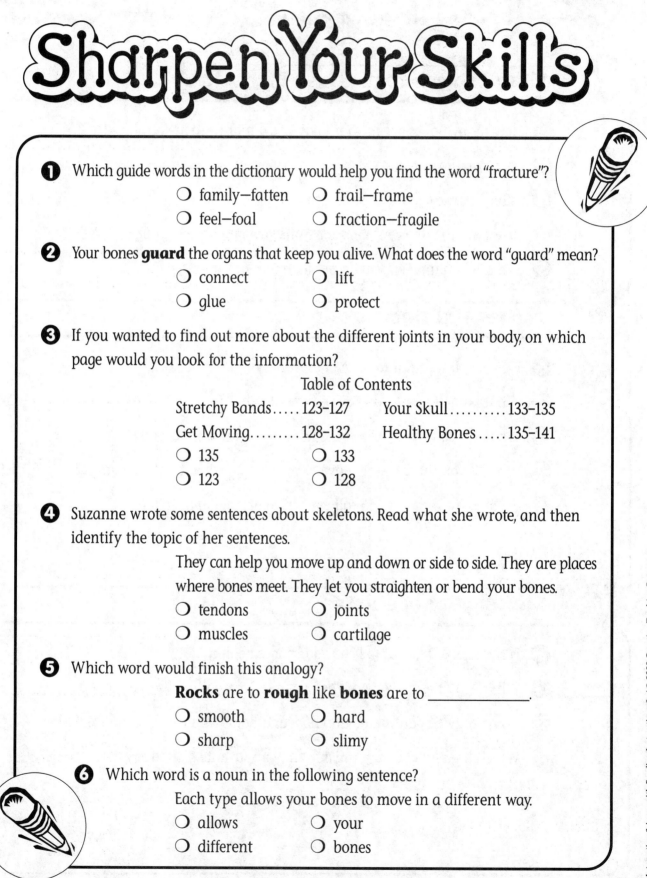

1 Which guide words in the dictionary would help you find the word "fracture"?

○ family–fatten   ○ frail–frame

○ feel–foal   ○ fraction–fragile

2 Your bones **guard** the organs that keep you alive. What does the word "guard" mean?

○ connect   ○ lift

○ glue   ○ protect

3 If you wanted to find out more about the different joints in your body, on which page would you look for the information?

Table of Contents

Stretchy Bands.....123–127   Your Skull..........133–135

Get Moving.........128–132   Healthy Bones.....135–141

○ 135   ○ 133

○ 123   ○ 128

4 Suzanne wrote some sentences about skeletons. Read what she wrote, and then identify the topic of her sentences.

They can help you move up and down or side to side. They are places where bones meet. They let you straighten or bend your bones.

○ tendons   ○ joints

○ muscles   ○ cartilage

5 Which word would finish this analogy?

Rocks are to **rough** like **bones** are to _____.

○ smooth   ○ hard

○ sharp   ○ slimy

6 Which word is a noun in the following sentence?

Each type allows your bones to move in a different way.

○ allows   ○ your

○ different   ○ bones

Integrating Science with Reading Instruction · 3–4 © 2002 Creative Teaching Press

James, Marcus, Tarek, and Gwen are doing a report on skeletons. Each student chose one topic to focus on. Use the clues below to decide which topic each student chose.

Clues

1 Tarek learned more about strong, stretchy bands that connect bones together.

2 Marcus did not do more research on muscles or tendons.

3 Gwen learned that her heart is one of these.

4 James learned about what attaches muscles to bones.

	James	Marcus	Tarek	Gwen
Muscles				
Joints				
Tendons				
Ligaments				

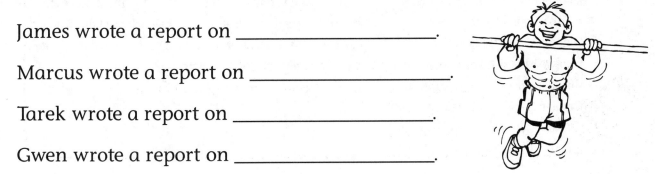

James wrote a report on _____.

Marcus wrote a report on _____.

Tarek wrote a report on _____.

Gwen wrote a report on _____.

Our Skeleton

What makes the skeleton strong enough to support the body?

Teacher Background Information

The skeleton provides a lightweight but very strong framework for the body. It gives the body shape and support. Ounce for ounce, your bones are stronger than steel or reinforced concrete. Many long bones in the body have a round or columnar shape. Round columns are much stronger than rectangular- or triangular-shaped columns because they distribute the weight evenly and there are no weak spots. A lot of mineral matter, especially calcium phosphate, has been deposited between the living cells. This forms the outer portion of the bone, called compact bone, which is quite hard. It is important for children to drink milk because the calcium in milk helps to build strong and healthy bones and teeth. The inner part of the bone looks more like a honeycomb and is called spongy bone. Many bones are hollow in the center and have a soft tissue called marrow filling the inside area. Think of the bone like a straw. The center of the straw would be filled with marrow. This is why the skeleton is relatively lightweight. There are two kinds of marrow inside bones. Red marrow is found in the ends of long bones, in the vertebrae, and in flat bones like the ribs, breastbone, and shoulder blades. Yellow marrow is found in the shaft of long bones. Ask a butcher for marrow soup bones to complete this project with students.

Experiment Results

Have each student record his or her results on the Column Testing Chart (page 30). The round column will be the strongest of the three shapes because this allows the weight to be distributed more evenly. There will not be any weak spots. The number of books the round column can actually support may surprise the students. Many long bones have a round shape. It makes them much stronger. The outside of the bone will feel hard. The soft marrow fills the inside of the bone. The shape and flexibility of the bones provide added strength.

Integrating Science with Reading Instruction · 3–4 © 2002 Creative Teaching Press

Our Skeleton

What makes the skeleton strong enough to support the body?

Procedure

1 Fold one piece of construction paper lengthwise into thirds. Open it up, and tape the two edges together to create a triangle shape.

2 Fold another piece of construction paper lengthwise in half and then in half again. (This will give you four columns.) Open up the paper, and form it into a rectangular column. Tape the two edges together.

3 Form the last piece of construction paper lengthwise into a round column (cylinder). Overlap the edges a little bit, and tape them together.

4 Test each column for its weight-bearing strength. Stand each column upright and place a book on top of it. Keep adding books until the column collapses or the stack of books falls off.

5 Record your results on the Column Testing Chart.

6 Use the magnifying glass to look at a cross section of the bone with marrow. Notice the shape of the bone. Feel the hard bone tissue, and notice where the marrow is located. Feel the marrow, if you would like to. Wash your hands when you finish.

MATERIALS

(per group)
- ✔ Column Testing Chart (page 30)
- ✔ 3 pieces of 9" x 12" (23 cm x 30.5 cm) construction paper
- ✔ tape
- ✔ stack of books
- ✔ magnifying glass
- ✔ cross section of a round bone with marrow

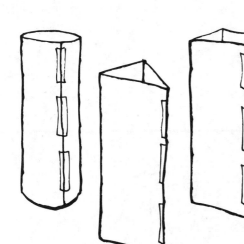

Column Testing Chart

Directions: Test each type of column, and write the number of books it supported without falling down.

Shape of Column Tested	Number of Books It Supported
Triangular Column	
Rectangular Column	
Round Column	

Integrating Science with Reading Instruction · 3–4 © 2002 Creative Teaching Press

Name _____   Date _____

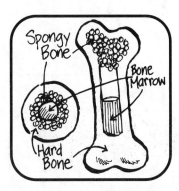

Our Skeleton

What makes the skeleton strong enough to support the body?

Results and Conclusions

1 Which shape was the strongest column?

_____

2 What shape was the bone you observed? _____
Why do you think a lot of bones are shaped like this?

_____

3 How did the outside part of the bone feel?

_____

4 What was inside the bone? _____
How is it different from the outside part of the bone?

_____

5 Can you give two reasons why the bones of the skeleton are so strong and yet lightweight?

_____

6 What makes the skeleton strong enough to support the body?

_____

Integrating Science with Reading Instruction · 3–4 © 2002 Creative Teaching Press

Catch a Clue

What will we learn about in our reading today?

solar system

community

food chains

ocean life

Our Clues

1. We are a part of one.

2. It must be balanced.

3. It relies on the sun.

4. Every part depends on the others to live.

Integrating Science with Reading Instruction · 3–4 © 2002 Creative Teaching Press

Concept Map

Facts we already know about **food chains,** and the new facts we have learned

Food Chains

Integrating Science with Reading Instruction · 3–4 © 2002 Creative Teaching Press

Word Warm-Up

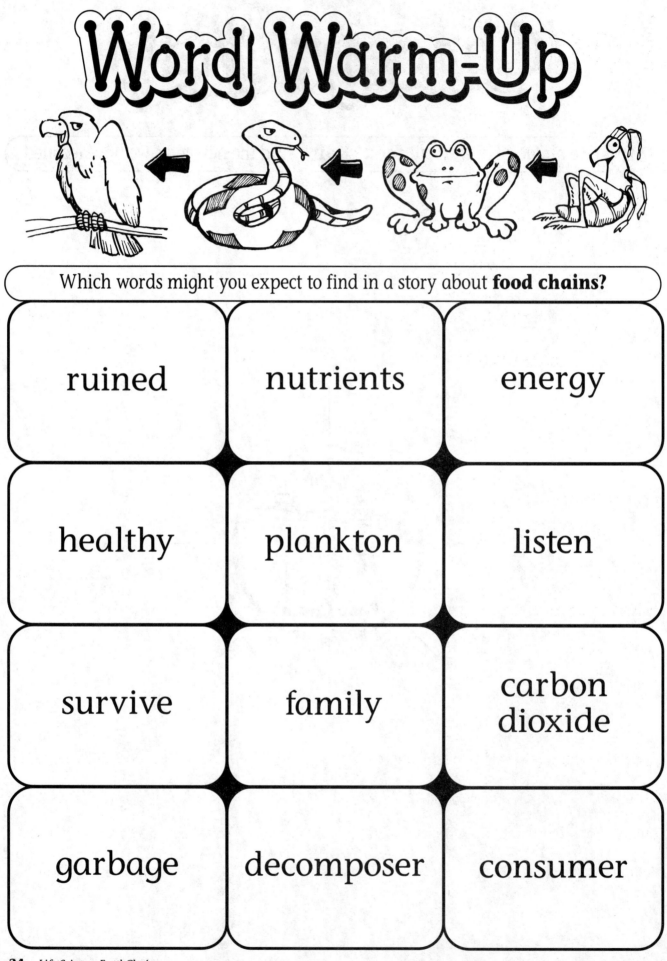

Which words might you expect to find in a story about **food chains?**

ruined	nutrients	energy
healthy	plankton	listen
survive	family	carbon dioxide
garbage	decomposer	consumer

Integrating Science with Reading Instruction · 3–4 © 2002 Creative Teaching Press

Food Chains

What is a food chain? A food chain explains how living things eat other living things in order to stay alive. All living things are linked to each other. They need other living things to survive. A food chain is like a ladder. Imagine you are standing in the middle of a ladder. You would eat the animals or plants that are below you on the ladder. The animals above you on the ladder would eat you!

The sun is needed in a food chain. It gives plants and animals the energy to grow. There would not be a food chain at all without sunlight.

All food chains begin with a link called a producer. Producers make food from nonliving things. A green plant is an example of a producer. Have you ever watered a plant? If so, you have helped a plant make its own food! The plant takes that water and uses the sun's energy to combine it with carbon dioxide. This is how the plant makes its own food. This gives the plant nourishment. It is just like when you eat a healthy meal.

The next link in a food chain is called a consumer. A consumer is any living thing that needs a producer for food. There are many types of consumers. One type is called an herbivore. This is an animal that only eats plants. A plant gets nutrients from the food it makes. Then, an animal gets nourishment by eating the plant. The second type of consumer is called a carnivore. Animals that only eat other animals are called carnivores. The third type of consumer is called

Integrating Science with Reading Instruction · 3–4 © 2002 Creative Teaching Press

an omnivore. Animals and people who eat both plants and animals are called omnivores. What type of consumer are you?

The last link in a food chain is called a decomposer. Decomposers, like bacteria and fungi, are living things that eat dead plants and animals or help them decay. Decomposers are nature's garbage collectors. They help to keep the earth clean and healthy. Can you imagine what the earth would look like if each plant and animal that died just laid on the ground forever? It would be a very crowded and stinky world! You can see that even though most decomposers are small, they do a very big job.

Let's look at a food chain in action in the sea. At the bottom of the food chain, there are plants and plankton. Fish and animals like shrimp, jellyfish, and sea stars need to eat this plankton to live. Then, larger fish like tuna and mackerel eat the jellyfish and shrimp. Then, even larger fish and animals such as sharks, seals, and people eat them. Do you know what would happen if all of the plankton disappeared? The shrimp and jellyfish would die because they would not have any food. So, the tuna and mackerel would not have as much to eat, and they could start to die. If this went up the food chain, it could affect our lives as well. Just like each step on a ladder is important to make it to the top, we need each part of the food chain to keep the balance of life the same. This way all living things can survive!

Integrating Science with Reading Instruction · 3–4 © 2002 Creative Teaching Press

Comprehension Questions

? Literal Questions

1. What is a food chain?

2. What are the three links of a food chain?

3. What is a carnivore? An herbivore? An omnivore?

4. Why is the sun important to food chains?

5. Who or what would be high on a food chain? Who or what would be low?

? Inferential Questions

1. If all of the decomposers died, what would happen to the earth?

2. Why is a green plant a producer?

3. What do you think happens when an animal becomes extinct?

4. How do hunting, overcrowding, and the destruction of natural habitats affect a food chain?

5. How does a food chain directly affect your life?

? Making Connections

1. Where would you fit in a food chain?

2. What kind of consumer are you?

3. Why is a food chain important to humans?

4. What did you eat for breakfast today? How do these foods fit into a food chain?

Sharpen Your Skills

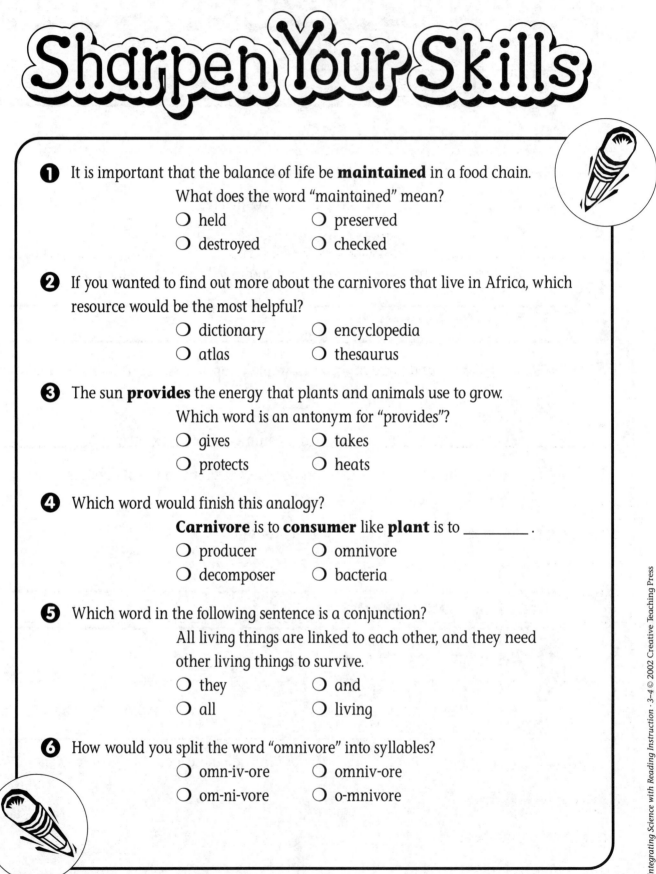

1 It is important that the balance of life be **maintained** in a food chain.
What does the word "maintained" mean?
- ○ held
- ○ preserved
- ○ destroyed
- ○ checked

2 If you wanted to find out more about the carnivores that live in Africa, which resource would be the most helpful?
- ○ dictionary
- ○ encyclopedia
- ○ atlas
- ○ thesaurus

3 The sun **provides** the energy that plants and animals use to grow.
Which word is an antonym for "provides"?
- ○ gives
- ○ takes
- ○ protects
- ○ heats

4 Which word would finish this analogy?
Carnivore is to **consumer** like **plant** is to _____ .
- ○ producer
- ○ omnivore
- ○ decomposer
- ○ bacteria

5 Which word in the following sentence is a conjunction?
All living things are linked to each other, and they need other living things to survive.
- ○ they
- ○ and
- ○ all
- ○ living

6 How would you split the word "omnivore" into syllables?
- ○ omn-iv-ore
- ○ omniv-ore
- ○ om-ni-vore
- ○ o-mnivore

Integrating Science with Reading Instruction · 3–4 © 2002 Creative Teaching Press

Name _____ Date _____

Shanelle, Colby, Calvin, and Elton wanted to learn more about the different elements of a food chain. Each student chose one area to learn about and teach the others. Read the clues below to decide which level of a food chain each student researched.

Clues

1 Calvin researched how a plant uses the sun's energy to combine water with carbon dioxide to make food.

2 Shanelle researched animals that are meat eaters.

3 Colby is a vegetarian and decided to research the level of a food chain that was similar to his eating habits.

4 Elton researched bacteria.

	Shanelle	Colby	Calvin	Elton
Herbivores				
Decomposers				
Producers				
Carnivores				

Shanelle researched _____.

Colby researched _____.

Calvin researched _____.

Elton researched _____.

Food Chains

Why is the order of a food chain important?

Teacher Background Information

Food chains illustrate the way energy is transferred within a segment of a particular environment. It does not matter whether you are looking at a desert, grassland, forest, tundra, aquatic (fresh water), or marine environment. There will be food chains in all of these locations. The basic components will be the same, too. Every food chain starts with a producer, which is some type of green plant. The plants will be eaten by primary consumers called herbivores. These animals will be eaten by secondary consumers called carnivores. There may or may not be omnivores in the chain. Finally, nature's decomposers cause the decay of the dead plants and animals and return useful nutrients to the environment. Then, the cycle starts over again. The green plants, represented in this project by leaves, use the energy of the sun to make their own food. The producers are then eaten by a caterpillar (an herbivore), which is then eaten by a spider (a carnivore). The spider is eaten by a bird (in this case an omnivore), which when it dies, supplies nourishment for the decomposers (the mushrooms, soil insects, and worms, as well as soil bacteria that are too small to see). Small plastic spiders are available at toy stores, hobby shops, party stores, and craft stores.

Experiment Results

The sun provides the energy for all food chains to begin, since green plants use the sun's energy to make food through the process of photosynthesis. If there were not enough producers in an environment, it would impact all the other members of the food chain, causing a decrease in their numbers, too. The number of steps in a food chain varies. The number of consumers varies from one environment to another. In general, most people are omnivores who eat plant and animal matter. You may have some students who are vegetarian and would be called herbivores. We do not notice the decomposers at work because most of them are very small, even microscopic.

Integrating Science with Reading Instruction · 3–4 © 2002 Creative Teaching Press

Food Chains

Why is the order of a food chain important?

Integrating Science with Reading Instruction · 3–4 © 2002 Creative Teaching Press

MATERIALS

(per student)

✔ What Is a Food Chain? reproducible (page 42)
✔ crayons or markers
✔ scissors
✔ glue
✔ 6 index cards
✔ cotton ball
✔ green pipe cleaner
✔ small plastic spider
✔ feather

Procedure

1 Color your reproducible, and cut out each square.

2 Glue each square onto a separate index card.

3 Glue a cotton ball onto the cloud shape.

4 Twist the pipe cleaner around a pencil. Slide it off. This curled pipe cleaner is a "caterpillar," an herbivore. Glue the caterpillar next to the leaf with a bite taken out of it.

5 Glue the plastic spider in the space given for a carnivore.

6 Glue the feather on the bird's tail.

7 Review the steps in a food chain with a partner in the following ways:

- Place the cards facedown. Then, have your partner time you for 20 seconds while you put the cards in order and try to beat the clock.

- Place the cards on the ground with one missing, and have your partner guess which part of the food chain is missing.

- Pick a food chain card. Show it to your partner. Ask your partner what the next card in the food chain would be.

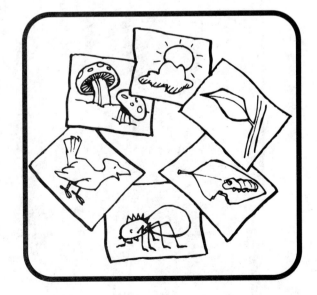

What Is a Food Chain?

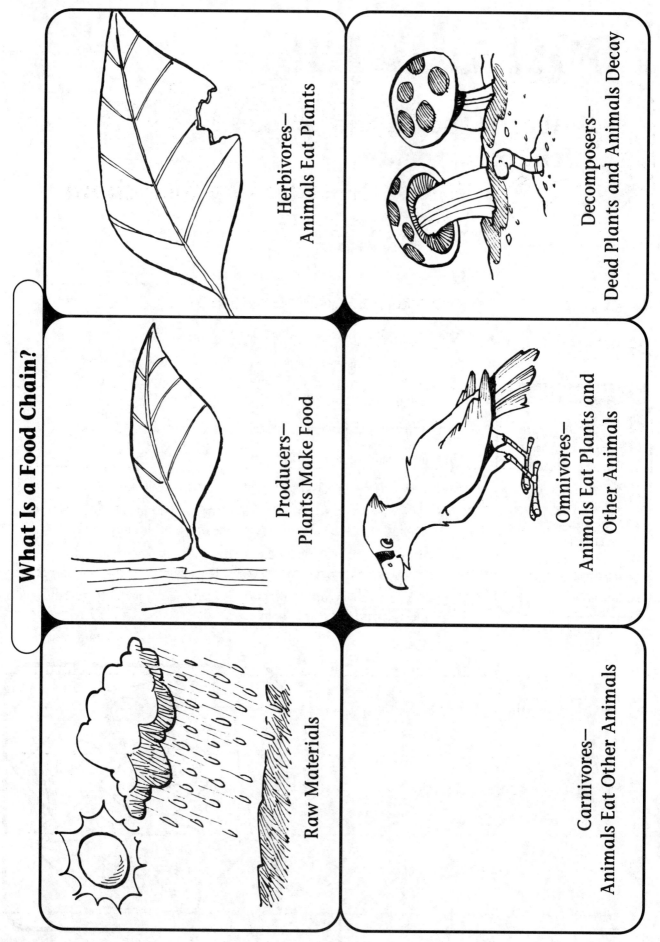

Herbivores—
Animals Eat Plants

Decomposers—
Dead Plants and Animals Decay

Producers—
Plants Make Food

Omnivores—
Animals Eat Plants and
Other Animals

Raw Materials

Carnivores—
Animals Eat Other Animals

Integrating Science with Reading Instruction ·3–4 © 2002 Creative Teaching Press

Name _____ Date _____

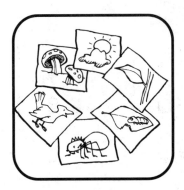

Food Chains

Why is the order of a food chain important?

Results and Conclusions

❶ Why is there a sun and rain cloud in the raw materials box?

_____

❷ Can you think of another animal that would fit in place of the caterpillar?

_____

❸ Do you think you could have a food chain with fewer steps? _____ More steps? _____
Why or why not?

_____

❹ Do you think the food chain would still work properly if you took out the producers? _____
Why or why not?

_____

❺ What do you think our earth would look like if there were not decomposers?

_____

❻ What kind of consumer are you?

_____

❼ Why is the order of a food chain important?

_____

Integrating Science with Reading Instruction · 3–4 © 2002 Creative Teaching Press

Catch a Clue

What will we learn about in our reading today?

oceans

clouds

mountains

rain forests

Our Clues

❶ They have different layers.

❷ Very little sunlight reaches the bottom layer.

❸ They are rapidly being destroyed.

❹ Many endangered plants and animals live there.

Integrating Science with Reading Instruction · 3–4 © 2002 Creative Teaching Press

Concept Map

Facts we already know about **rain forests,** and the new facts we have learned

Rain Forests

Word Warm-Up

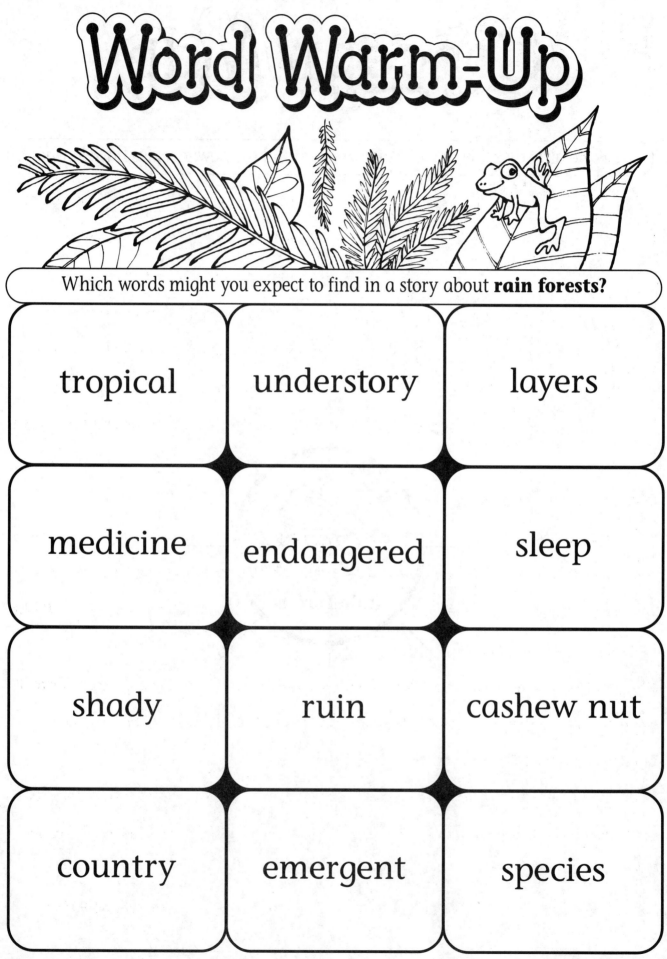

Which words might you expect to find in a story about **rain forests?**

tropical	understory	layers
medicine	endangered	sleep
shady	ruin	cashew nut
country	emergent	species

Integrating Science with Reading Instruction · 3–4 © 2002 Creative Teaching Press

Rain Forests

Rain forests are beautiful and helpful places. Plants and animals need rain forests. Did you know that half of the world's plant and animal groups live in the rain forests? Many of them are endangered. They need the rain forest to stay alive. We also need the rain forests. Have you eaten a banana, pineapple, coconut, or cashew nut? If so, you have eaten food that comes from a tropical rain forest. Have you ever needed medicine when you were sick? If so, then you may have used medicine that was made from plants in the rain forest.

Have you ever wondered what life is like in a tropical rain forest? Imagine you are near the Amazon River and you decided to walk through a tropical rain forest. You would see four layers as you look up toward the sky. They are the forest floor, understory, canopy, and emergent layer. Different types of plants and animals live in each layer.

You would walk on the lowest layer of the rain forest called the forest floor. It is shady there. It gets almost none of the day's sunlight. The tropical rain forest floor is made up of bare ground, dropped seeds and fruits, dead leaves, and branches.

If you looked up toward the sky, you would see the next layer called the understory. It is also pretty dark there. It does not get a lot of sunlight. Young trees and plants that do not need a lot of light live in this layer.

The next layer up is called the canopy layer. This layer has thick trees that rise 60–90 feet

Integrating Science with Reading Instruction · 3–4 © 2002 Creative Teaching Press

(18.3–27 meters) above the ground. That is as tall as a six-story building! The canopy treetops are close together, and the branches are covered with other plants and vines. This keeps a lot of sunlight from going deeper into the rain forest. Most living things live in this layer.

The top layer is called the emergent layer. Giant trees rise out of the top of the rain forest and into the sky. They get the most sunlight. They also have to live through a lot of heat and strong winds.

Did you know that $1\frac{1}{2}$ acres (.607 hectares) of trees are cut down in the rain forests every second? That means in just one minute, 90 acres (36.42 hectares) of trees are cut down! That is called deforestation. Scientists worry that we may lose all of the rain forests. This means all of the plants and animals that live there would die, too! Each species needs others to stay alive. When something is ruined in the rain forest, it affects other living things, too. During your next visit to the library, read a book to learn more about how you can help protect the rain forests and help save the plants and animals that live there.

Comprehension Questions

Integrating Science with Reading Instruction ·3–4 © 2002 Creative Teaching Press

? Literal Questions

1. What is deforestation?

2. Why is deforestation harmful?

3. What are the four layers of a tropical rain forest?

4. Where do most of the animals live in a rain forest?

5. What are some foods we get from tropical rain forests?

? Inferential Questions

1. Why does it get so much darker as you go from the top layers of a rain forest down to the floor?

2. Why do you think this environment is called a rain forest?

3. What would happen if one of the animals of a rain forest became extinct?

4. Compare the rain forest floor with the canopy layer. How are they the same? How are they different?

5. Why can so many different plants and animals live in a tropical rain forest?

? Making Connections

1. If you could travel to a tropical rain forest, what three things would you most want to see? Why?

2. Which layer of the rain forest is the most interesting to you? Why?

3. Draw a picture that shows the four layers of a tropical rain forest.

4. What can you do to help protect the life of a rain forest?

Name _____   Date _____

Sharpen Your Skills

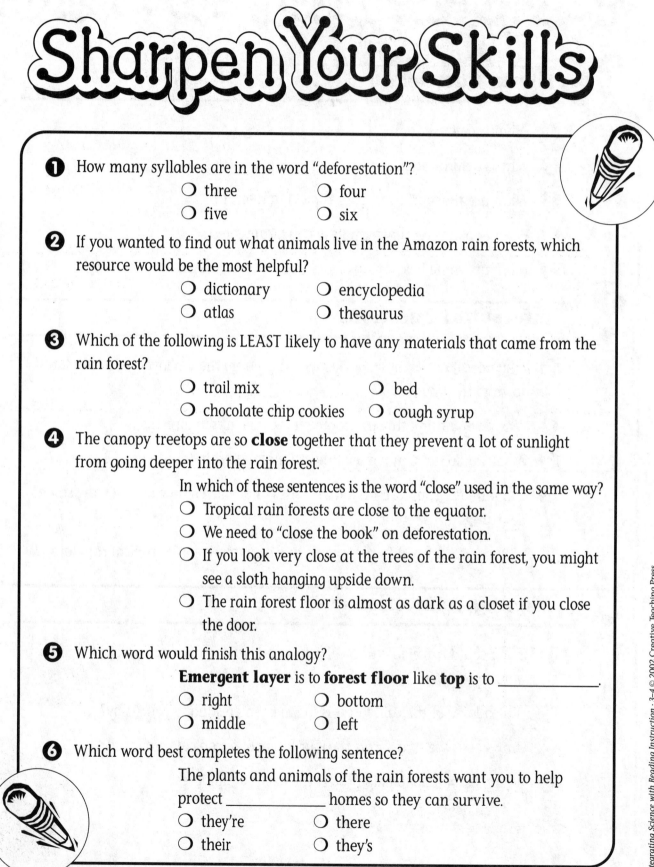

1 How many syllables are in the word "deforestation"?
- ○ three
- ○ four
- ○ five
- ○ six

2 If you wanted to find out what animals live in the Amazon rain forests, which resource would be the most helpful?
- ○ dictionary
- ○ encyclopedia
- ○ atlas
- ○ thesaurus

3 Which of the following is LEAST likely to have any materials that came from the rain forest?
- ○ trail mix
- ○ bed
- ○ chocolate chip cookies
- ○ cough syrup

4 The canopy treetops are so **close** together that they prevent a lot of sunlight from going deeper into the rain forest.

In which of these sentences is the word "close" used in the same way?
- ○ Tropical rain forests are close to the equator.
- ○ We need to "close the book" on deforestation.
- ○ If you look very close at the trees of the rain forest, you might see a sloth hanging upside down.
- ○ The rain forest floor is almost as dark as a closet if you close the door.

5 Which word would finish this analogy?

Emergent layer is to **forest floor** like **top** is to _____.
- ○ right
- ○ bottom
- ○ middle
- ○ left

6 Which word best completes the following sentence?

The plants and animals of the rain forests want you to help protect _____ homes so they can survive.
- ○ they're
- ○ there
- ○ their
- ○ they's

Integrating Science with Reading Instruction · 3–4 © 2002 Creative Teaching Press

Name _____   Date _____

Marcus, Pierre, Mary, and Penelope went on vacation to the Amazon rain forest. Each student loved to take pictures. The students decided they would each take pictures of everything that was interesting in one layer of the rain forest during their "Radical Rain Forest Tour." Use the clues below to decide which layer of the rain forest each student photographed.

Clues

1 Mary was worried because it was so dark that she did not think the pictures she took would turn out.

2 Marcus took some beautiful pictures of tall treetops, even though it was very windy.

3 Pierre's pictures were filled with lots of animals—many of which are endangered.

4 Many of Penelope's pictures show shady areas with young trees growing.

	Marcus	Pierre	Mary	Penelope
Emergent Layer				
Canopy Layer				
Understory				
Forest Floor				

Marcus took pictures while visiting the _____.

Pierre took pictures while visiting the _____.

Mary took pictures while visiting the _____.

Penelope took pictures while visiting the _____.

Integrating Science with Reading Instruction · 3–4 © 2002 Creative Teaching Press

Rain Forests

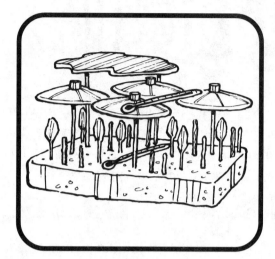

Why can so many different plants and animals live in a tropical rain forest?

Teacher Background Information

Before the class begins this experiment, discuss how a tropical rain forest grows in layers. Review the names (i.e., emergent, canopy, understory, and forest floor) and locations of the four layers. The canopy layer is the densest. The flat-crowned treetops grow so close to each other that canopy layer plants absorb most of the sunlight. Rain that goes through the canopy layer falls gently down on the understory and forest floor. Many plants grow on the branches of the canopy layer trees. These plants do not have their roots anchored in any soil. They attach themselves to the tree branches and absorb water from the humid air, as well as from the rain that falls. Also, many vines grow all over the canopy layer tree branches and tree trunks. Contrary to what you might think, tropical rain forest tree roots do not grow very deep in the soil. Instead, they spread out laterally, close to the surface. This allows them to absorb water very quickly when it rains. Some of the trees that reach up to the canopy and emergent layers have thick buttressed bases or extra stilt roots that help to support them.

Experiment Results

The room temperature at the beginning of the experiment will vary depending on the time of year students complete this activity. The temperature of the emergent layer should increase a few degrees (at least) after you shine your "sun" for 3–4 minutes. However, the temperature on the forest floor will have changed less. In the real forest, the forest floor temperature would stay fairly constant during the day. You would find different types of plants and animals in each layer of the rain forest because of the difference in the amount of sunlight, wind, and water. Plants that need the most sun would be in the emergent and canopy layers. Plants that grow in the shade would be found in the understory and even more so on the forest floor. The emergent layer gets the strongest winds because the very tall trees stick out of the top of the forest and are more exposed. The canopy layer supports the most animals because more plants are growing there and there are more places for animals to make their home (e.g., along vines and branches, in trees, and on flowers).

Integrating Science with Reading Instruction · 3–4 © 2002 Creative Teaching Press

Rain Forests

Why can so many different plants and animals live in a tropical rain forest?

Procedure

Integrating Science with Reading Instruction · 3–4 © 2002 Creative Teaching Press

1 Cut one brown pipe cleaner into 5–7 small pieces, and insert them into the Styrofoam block to represent plants on the forest floor.

2 Cut each green pipe cleaner into four pieces. Insert them into various places in the Styrofoam to represent understory trees.

3 Open the paper umbrellas, and insert them into the Styrofoam so that they overlap. These represent a canopy of "umbrella" trees.

4 Fold the other brown pipe cleaner in half, and twist the two pieces together. Bend the twisted pipe cleaners at the top to form an upside-down "L" shape. Cut an oval-shaped treetop from the green construction paper, and tape the treetop to the bent part of the pipe cleaner. This represents an emergent layer tree.

5 Carefully insert the pipe cleaner "tree" into the Styrofoam so that the "trunk" is between two umbrellas.

6 Place one small thermometer between the trees on the "forest floor," and gently lay the other thermometer on the umbrella trees. Read and record the temperature of this thermometer (room temperature) on a piece of paper.

7 Darken the room as much as possible. Hold the lamp 4–6 inches (10–15 cm) above the rain forest model. Turn on the lamp (or "sun"), and shine it on the emergent layer tree and the canopy layer umbrella trees.

8 Observe the amount of "sunlight" hitting the emergent layer and canopy layer. Observe from the side the amount of sunlight passing through to the forest floor.

9 Keep the light on for 3–4 minutes. (Take turns holding the light with other group members.)

10 Read the thermometer on the canopy layer tree. Turn off the lamp and read the thermometer on the forest floor. Record the results on your piece of paper.

MATERIALS

(per group)

- ✔ scissors
- ✔ 2 brown pipe cleaners
- ✔ 2 green "bump chenile" pipe cleaners
- ✔ 4" x 6" (10 cm x 15 cm) rectangular block of Styrofoam
- ✔ 5–6 paper "drink" umbrellas
- ✔ 2" (5 cm) green construction paper square
- ✔ tape
- ✔ 2 small glass thermometers
- ✔ lamp with 100 watt bulb
- ✔ lined paper

Rain Forests

Why can so many different plants and animals live in a tropical rain forest?

Results and Conclusions

1 What was the room temperature at the beginning of this experiment?

_____

2 How much "sunlight" reached the emergent layer and canopy layer?

_____

3 How much "sunlight" reached the forest floor?

_____

4 What was the temperature in the canopy layer after 3–4 minutes of sunlight?

_____

5 What was the temperature on the forest floor after 3–4 minutes of sunlight?

_____

6 In a real rain forest, the floor would be 60–70 feet (18.3–27 meters) below the canopy. How would this affect the temperature difference between the layers?

_____

7 Do you think the same kinds of plants and animals would live in the different layers of a rain forest? _____ Why or why not?

_____

8 In which layer(s) would you expect to find plants that need a lot of sun?

_____

9 In which layer(s) would you expect to find plants that grow in the shade?

_____

10 Why can so many different plants and animals live in a tropical rain forest?

_____

Integrating Science with Reading Instruction · 3–4 © 2002 Creative Teaching Press

Catch a Clue

What will we learn about in our reading today?

tornadoes

sound waves

earthquakes

space exploration

Our Clues

1 Most occur over our oceans.

2 They are a result of vibrations.

3 They can cause some damage.

4 They are difficult to predict.

Integrating Science with Reading Instruction · 3–4 © 2002 Creative Teaching Press

Concept Map

Facts we already know about **earthquakes,** and the new facts we have learned

Earthquakes

Integrating Science with Reading Instruction · 3–4 © 2002 Creative Teaching Press

Word Warm-Up

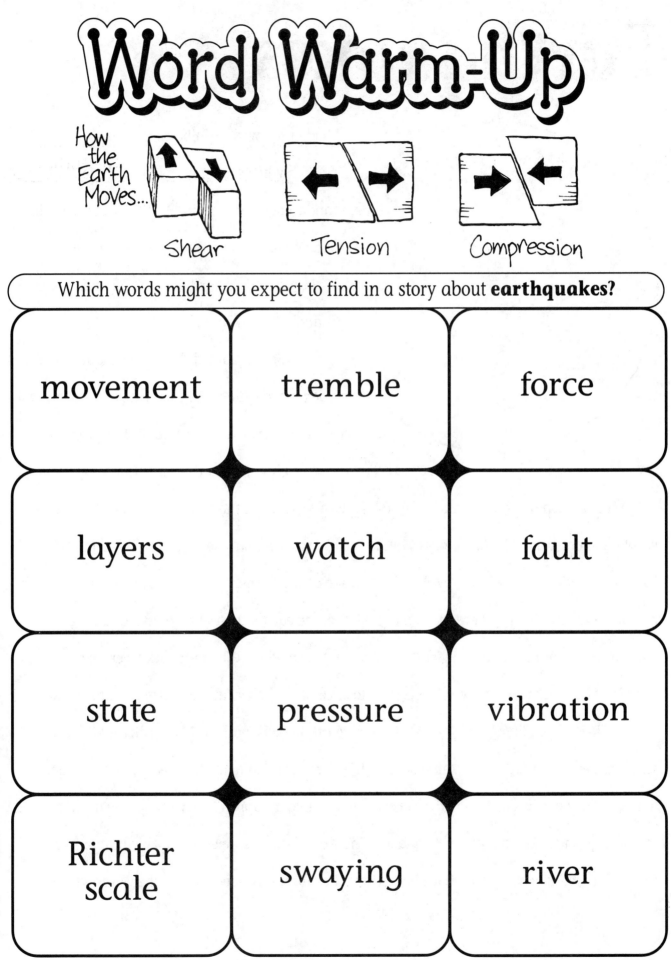

How the Earth Moves...

Shear

Tension

Compression

Which words might you expect to find in a story about **earthquakes?**

movement	tremble	force
layers	watch	fault
state	pressure	vibration
Richter scale	swaying	river

Earthquakes

I had just moved to California. I was sitting in my classroom when suddenly the room started to shake and things were moving. I felt like I was rocking on a boat. When it stopped, my teacher said we just had an earthquake. "What is an earthquake?" I asked.

She explained that an earthquake is a sudden movement of the earth's crust. "Have you ever been so cold that you began to shake or tremble?" she asked. My teacher explained that this same thing happens to the earth when there is too much force on the layers of rock in the earth. The crust of the earth is not all in one piece. There are places in the earth's crust that have large cracks called faults. Faults are made when the rock layers are not strong enough. They break because there is too much pressure on them. This makes sudden movements of the earth's crust. This pressure can cause the rock layers to move apart, push together, or slide past each other. When the rock layers move, a force is let go that makes the rock layers vibrate forcefully. The vibrations create an earthquake.

"How do you know when there will be an earthquake?" I asked. My teacher said that scientists keep trying to answer this question. It is hard for them to tell *when* earthquakes might happen. They have a good idea of *where* earthquakes might happen. They use special devices called seismographs to find out about earthquakes. These devices measure earthquake vibrations, or shock waves. The shock waves recorded tell how strong the vibrations were, how far the waves went, and

Integrating Science with Reading Instruction · 3–4 © 2002 Creative Teaching Press

how far away the center of the earthquake was from where the scientists are. Then, they know the exact place of the earthquake.

"How do people know the strength of an earthquake?" I asked. My teacher said it is measured on a Richter scale. She said to think of this scale from one to ten. One would be small and ten would be huge! Each number is worth ten times more than the number before it. That means that an earthquake that measures 7.0 is ten times stronger than an earthquake that measures 6.0 on the Richter scale. An earthquake that measures a 2.0 is just strong enough for you to feel. An earthquake that measures 5.0 can cause some damage. And, an earthquake that registers 7.0 or more is considered a major earthquake.

Now I was curious. I wondered what I should do if there was another earthquake. My teacher said we should "duck and cover." She showed us how to get under something that is strong and solid like a table or desk. We were told to cover our head and neck with our hands. Our teacher also said to stand in a doorway if there was not anything strong to get under. She reminded us to stay away from windows, mirrors, and shelves. Also, we were told to follow our school's safety rules during an earthquake drill so that we would know what to do. This made me feel better. Now I know what an earthquake is and what to do to be safe during one.

Comprehension Questions

? Literal Questions

1 What is an earthquake?

2 How is a fault made?

3 What are some safety tips to follow during an earthquake?

4 What is used to measure the vibrations of an earthquake?

5 What is used to measure the strength of an earthquake?

? Inferential Questions

1 How can you find out if an earthquake was mild or strong?

2 Why does the earth have earthquakes?

3 Why do you think it is hard for scientists to tell *when* an earthquake will happen?

4 Compare a 3.5 earthquake with a 5.5 earthquake. What do you think each would be like?

5 If scientists estimate that there are possibly 800,000 earthquakes each year, why don't you feel all of them?

? Making Connections

1 Have you ever felt an earthquake before? If so, what do you remember doing? If not, how would you feel?

2 If you were in bed sleeping during an earthquake, what would you do?

3 What supplies would be good to have in an earthquake preparedness kit?

4 Using your five senses, describe what you would probably experience in an 8.0 earthquake.

Integrating Science with Reading Instruction · 3–4 © 2002 Creative Teaching Press

Name _____ Date _____

Sharpen Your Skills

1 A seismograph records vibrations. A telegraph records electrical signals. An autograph is someone's signature.

What do you think the root word "graph" means?
- ○ to walk
- ○ to write
- ○ to figure
- ○ to read

2 Faults are created when the rock layers are not strong enough and break due to **extreme** pressure.

Which word is a synonym for "extreme"?
- ○ delicate
- ○ severe
- ○ mild
- ○ swaying

3 If you wanted to find out where the Pacific Ocean is, which resource would be the most helpful?
- ○ dictionary
- ○ encyclopedia
- ○ atlas
- ○ thesaurus

4 Which of the following does <u>not</u> belong on an earthquake preparedness list?

a. Buy a flashlight and batteries.

b. Make an escape plan.

c. Buy bottled water.

d. Find a safe place to hide near a window.
- ○ a
- ○ c
- ○ b
- ○ d

5 Which word would finish this analogy?

Clock is to **time** like **seismograph** is to _____.
- ○ vibrations
- ○ sways
- ○ sound waves
- ○ devices

6 How would you split the word "earthquake" into syllables?
- ○ ea-rthqua-ke
- ○ earth-quake
- ○ earthq-ua-ke
- ○ ear-thquak-e

Get Logical

Jennifer, Brenton, Linda, and Richard each had an earthquake in their hometown last year. Use the clues below to decide what the strength of each earthquake was on the Richter scale.

Clues

❶ Richard did not feel the earthquake, although he heard about it on the news. There were no reports of any damage.

❷ Jennifer was asleep when the earthquake occurred. She woke up right away. She saw things falling off the shelves and felt strong jolts. She stood in her doorway with her dad. The news said that a building collapsed.

❸ The earthquake in Linda's town was ten times stronger than the earthquake in Richard's town.

❹ Brenton felt the earthquake while he was at school. Everyone had to duck and cover and then evacuate. There was no visible damage.

	Jennifer	Brenton	Linda	Richard
2.0				
7.0				
3.0				
4.5				

The earthquake in Jennifer's town measured _____.

The earthquake in Brenton's town measured _____.

The earthquake in Linda's town measured _____.

The earthquake in Richard's town measured _____.

Integrating Science with Reading Instruction · 3–4 © 2002 Creative Teaching Press

Earthquakes

What causes earthquakes, and which way(s) can the ground move?

Teacher Background Information

The earth's crust is made of large sections called crustal plates. They fit together like pieces of a jigsaw puzzle. However, the heat and pressure in the layer below the crust, called the mantle, always make the crust move. Normally, the crustal plates move very slowly (about 1–2" or 2.5–5 cm a year) and the movement is not noticeable. When there is a sudden movement, we feel that as an earthquake. The crust's plates can move in three different ways. If the plates are pulled apart, this is called tension. This is what is happening along the floor of the Atlantic Ocean at the mid-Atlantic Ridge. The crust is actually getting larger there. If the plate pieces are pushed together, this is called compression. This can cause mountains to slowly build, such as the Andes in South America. Or, the plates can slide past each other in a sideways direction. This is called shear. This is the type of movement that occurs along the San Andreas Fault in California. All three types of movement can cause earthquakes.

Experiment Results

The crustal plates move sideways, sliding past each other. This is called shear. The students should observe some of the trees and houses falling over and perhaps even a crack in the soil surface. The most damage should occur near the junction of the two pieces of material, which represent the edges of the crustal plates. More movement occurs at these edges, or faults. This is where earthquakes occur.

Earthquakes

What causes earthquakes, and which way(s) can the ground move?

Procedure

1 Place the strips of cloth side by side in the box or tray. (Keep the ends hanging off the end of the container.) Each strip represents a crustal plate.

2 Fill the container with a mixture of soil and sand about 1–2" (2.5–5 cm) thick.

3 Sprinkle water over the top of the soil and sand to moisten it, and then press it down.

4 Arrange toy houses, twigs, and pipe cleaner trees over the surface of the soil and sand.

5 With a partner, pull the ends of the strips away from each other very slowly for about 2–4" (5–10 cm) so the strips slide past each other. Observe what happens.

6 Can you think of another way to arrange the pieces of material to show another type of earthquake? Try it.

MATERIALS

(per group)

✔ 2 strips of cloth (a little longer than the container)

✔ sturdy shallow box or plastic tray

✔ soil

✔ sand

✔ water

✔ small toy houses, twigs, pipe cleaner "trees"

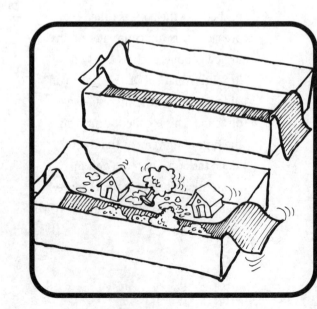

Integrating Science with Reading Instruction · 3–4 © 2002 Creative Teaching Press

Name _____   Date _____

 # Earthquakes

What causes earthquakes, and which way(s) can the ground move?

Results and Conclusions

❶ Which way did the "crustal plates" move in this experiment?

_____

What is this type of movement called?

_____

❷ What did you observe during your "earthquake"?

_____

❸ How were the houses and trees affected?

_____

❹ Where was the most damage?

_____

Why?

_____

❺ What causes earthquakes, and which way(s) can the ground move?

_____

Catch a Clue

What will we learn about in our reading today?

volcanoes

earthquakes

rocks

meteor showers

Our Clues

1 They are as old as our history.

2 They can cause a great deal of damage and are hard to predict.

3 They are on earth and in space.

4 Some islands were created by them.

Integrating Science with Reading Instruction · 3–4 © 2002 Creative Teaching Press

Concept Map

Facts we already know about **volcanoes,** and the new facts we have learned

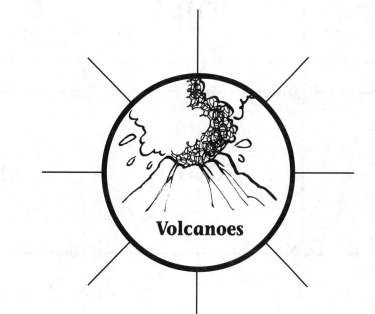

Volcanoes

Word Warm-Up

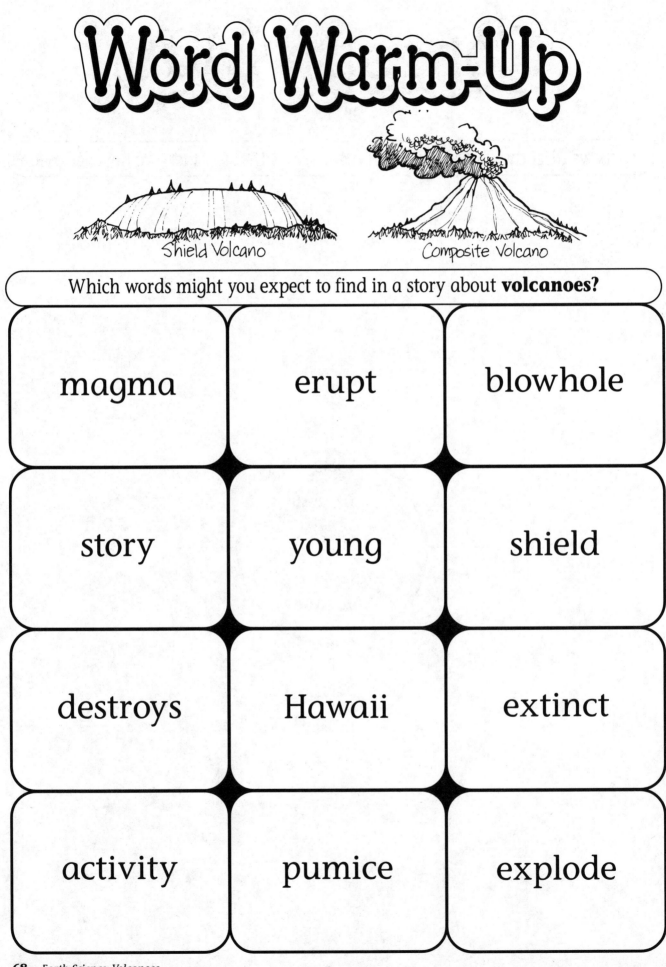

Shield Volcano   Composite Volcano

Which words might you expect to find in a story about **volcanoes?**

magma	erupt	blowhole
story	young	shield
destroys	Hawaii	extinct
activity	pumice	explode

Integrating Science with Reading Instruction · 3–4 © 2002 Creative Teaching Press

Volcanoes

How do volcanoes form? A volcano forms when magma (melted rock deep in the earth), gases, and rocks erupt through openings in the earth's crust. The magma that erupts out of the volcano onto the earth is called lava.

There are three types of volcanoes. The first type is called a composite volcano. This type is explosive. When it explodes, lava, ash, and gases shoot out of an opening in it. To imagine what this looks like, think about the spray that shoots up from a whale's blowhole. The volcano shoots up in the same way but on a much larger scale and a lot hotter. Hardened lava and ash build up over the years. They can form mountains that are quite tall. Mount St. Helens (located in the state of Washington) is a composite volcano.

Some volcanoes do not shoot lava up in the air. The lava pours out of it instead. When the lava gets to the surface of the earth, it moves like a thick river. This type of volcano is called a shield volcano. The lava flows slowly over the land. It destroys anything in its path. But you do not have to worry! The lava moves slowly enough for people who live nearby to leave safely. Then, the lava flow slows down, cools off, and turns into rock. Shield volcanoes form shorter mountains. They are wide, rounded, and smooth. If you visit Hawaii, look for some shield volcanoes. You will find them there!

The third type of volcano forms quickly and is smaller. It is called a cinder cone volcano. These volcanoes are usually less than 300–400 feet (91.5–122 meters) tall. They explode one time quickly. When cinder cones erupt, they force out ash, gases, and lava in tiny bits.

Integrating Science with Reading Instruction · 3–4 © 2002 Creative Teaching Press

After a volcano erupts, the lava cools off. It gets hard and becomes igneous rock. How the volcano erupts determines the kind of igneous rock that is formed. Composite volcanoes form rocks from the lava that shoots out of it. Some of these rocks are obsidian and pumice. Magma that gets trapped in the earth's crust forms granite. Shield volcanoes make rocks such as basalt, "pahoehoe," and "aa" (pronounced "ah-ah"). The last two names are Hawaiian. The "pahoehoe" rock feels like rope. The "aa" is a sharp and jagged rock. Tuff, pumice, and lots of basalt cinders come from cinder cone volcanoes. Pumice is made from lava that has many bubbles of hot gases in it. The lava cools so fast that the gases do not have time to get out. Some pieces of pumice are so full of holes from the gases that they can float in water!

Volcanoes have been forming for thousands of years. Some are still active. This means that they have erupted in the last 10,000 years and could erupt again. Others are dormant or extinct. Dormant volcanoes show no signs of activity. Many scientists think they could erupt again some day. Those that are extinct have not had any signs of activity in the last 10,000 years. They probably will not erupt again.

Integrating Science with Reading Instruction · 3–4 © 2002 Creative Teaching Press

Comprehension Questions

? Literal Questions

1. What are the three types of volcanoes?

2. What kind of volcano explodes with lava, ash, and gases?

3. What type of volcanoes are on the islands of Hawaii?

4. What type of volcano has lava that moves like a thick river?

5. What is lava? How does it change form?

? Inferential Questions

1. Compare and contrast composite and cinder cone volcanoes. How are they the same? How are they different?

2. Why do volcanoes erupt?

3. Can every volcano erupt at any time? Why or why not?

4. Our earth has limited land space. If we needed to build more homes, which volcanoes would be the safest to build near? Why?

5. Why do volcanoes make many different kinds of igneous rocks?

? Making Connections

1. Where is the closest volcano to where you live? What kind of volcano is it?

2. How is a volcano the same as a garden hose with an attachment that varies the amount of water that comes out?

3. Would you want to live in a three-story mansion with eight bedrooms and a pool if it were at the base of a cinder cone volcano? Why or why not?

4. If you wanted to learn more about a certain type of volcano, which one would you choose? Why?

Name _____   Date _____

Sharpen Your Skills

1 If you put these words in alphabetical order, which word would come third?

○ crust   ○ composite

○ crater   ○ cinder

2 If you wanted to find out the definition of the word "composite," which resource would be the most helpful?

○ dictionary   ○ encyclopedia

○ atlas   ○ thesaurus

3 A volcano is formed when magma, gases, and rocks erupt **through** openings in the earth's crust.

In which of these sentences is the word "through" used in the same way?

○ Through the years, many volcanoes have become dormant.

○ When the lava is through flowing, then it will harden into lava rock.

○ Composite volcanoes shoot lava through the air when they erupt.

○ Scientists are studying volcanic activity through different methods.

4 Composite and cinder cones are **two** different types of volcanoes. Shield volcanoes are another type, **too.**

The words "two" and "too" are _____.

○ synonyms   ○ antonyms

○ homophones   ○ homographs

5 Which word is an adjective in the following sentence?

Pumice is made from lava that had many hot gases in it.

○ pumice   ○ hot

○ gases   ○ made

6 How would you split the word "volcanic" into syllables?

○ volc-ani-c   ○ vol-ca-nic

○ vol-c-an-ic   ○ vol-can-ic

Integrating Science with Reading Instruction · 3–4 © 2002 Creative Teaching Press

Name _____ Date _____

Get Logical

Jonah, Rosie, and Lorraine wanted to make volcanoes for the science fair. Each student chose to read about and create a different type of volcano. Use the clues below to decide what kind of volcano each student made.

Clues

1 Lorraine's volcano erupted straight up into the air! What a mess!

2 The lava slowly flowed out over the sides of Rosie's volcano.

3 Jonah was having a hard time making lava in tiny bits shoot out of his volcano.

	Jonah	Rosie	Lorraine
Shield Volcano			
Composite Volcano			
Cinder Cone Volcano			

Jonah made a _____.

Rosie made a _____.

Lorraine made a _____.

Volcanoes

Why do volcanoes make several types of igneous rocks?

Teacher Background Information

Igneous rocks form when tremendous heat and pressure in the mantle force some magma into or on top of the earth's crust. The magma that is forced onto the earth's crust is known as lava. There are two main types of igneous rocks. Those formed from lava are called extrusive rocks (e.g., obsidian, pumice, basalt), and those formed from magma trapped inside the earth's crust are called intrusive rocks (e.g., granite). The main difference between the two types is related to how fast or slow the rocks cool and harden. The igneous rocks made from lava cool quickly and have very small or no visible crystals. The igneous rocks made from magma that was trapped inside the earth's crust cool slowly and have large, easily visible crystals. The depth and temperature of the magma also influences the type of rocks formed. Magma that originates from deeper chambers in the earth will have a higher gas and water content than magma that was closer to the surface.

Different minerals in the magma form crystals at different temperatures. Several different kinds of rocks can be created from a few basic mineral ingredients. You can buy vermiculite from a plant nursery. Quick-set plaster hardens in about 20–30 minutes. Do not allow students to wash their hands at the sink if they have plaster on them. It will harden inside the pipes! Ask students to wash their hands first in a bucket and then wash them again at the sink.

Experiment Results

Have each student record his or her results on the Igneous Rock Chart (page 76). If students observed samples of igneous rocks, they will notice that all of the rocks feel hard. The rocks are all shades of darker or drab colors (no bright colors). The rock samples are different in their surface texture. Obsidian is a glassy rock, whereas basalt and pumice will be dull and usually have some holes in them. The granite will have a speckled appearance. After making their own igneous rocks, students will see that different mixtures of materials in the magma or lava will result in different types of igneous rocks. They might also see that the amount of gas trapped in the magma could vary, as well as the temperature.

Integrating Science with Reading Instruction · 3–4 © 2002 Creative Teaching Press

Volcanoes

Why do volcanoes make several types of igneous rocks?

Integrating Science with Reading Instruction · 3–4 © 2002 Creative Teaching Press

MATERIALS

(per group)

- ✔ Igneous Rock Chart (page 76)
- ✔ magnifying glass
- ✔ samples of obsidian, basalt, pumice, and granite (optional)
- ✔ newspaper
- ✔ small bowl of dry quick-set Plaster of Paris
- ✔ measuring cup
- ✔ bowl
- ✔ 5 plastic spoons
- ✔ 3 small containers
- ✔ vermiculite
- ✔ sand
- ✔ black tempera paint (powdered or liquid)
- ✔ 4 paper cups
- ✔ pitcher of water
- ✔ bucket of soapy water

Procedure

1. Look at the samples of igneous rock with a magnifying glass. Observe the color, texture, and presence of visible crystals. Discuss their similarities and differences with your group. (Skip this step if there are no rock samples.)

2. Cover your table with newspaper. Place 2 cups of plaster into the bowl. Put a spoon in the bowl.

3. Put vermiculite in one small container, sand in another, and black tempera paint in the third container. Place a spoon in each container so you can spoon these ingredients into the cups.

4. Fill each paper cup halfway full of dry plaster.

5. Add different combinations of vermiculite, sand, and/or black tempera paint to each cup. You can add one or more ingredients, and you can change the amount you add. For example, add to the first cup of plaster one part vermiculite and two parts black tempera paint or add one part sand, one part vermiculite, and one part black tempera paint. (Be sure to use a different combination for each cup.)

6. Add just enough water to each paper cup to make the mixture like thick cream. Stir each mixture with a spoon. Remove the spoons and throw them away.

7. Allow your "igneous rocks" to cool and harden for 20 minutes. (The cups will feel warm after you first mix in the water.)

8. While you are waiting for your rocks to cool and harden, clean up your table. Wash your hands <u>first</u> in the bucket of soapy water. Then, wash your hands again at the sink.

9. After 20 minutes, tear away the paper cups. This will reveal your igneous rocks.

10. Record your results on your Igneous Rock Chart.

Name _____

Date _____

Directions: Place a check in the appropriate boxes to show which ingredients you used to create each "rock." You can show how much of an ingredient you added by using tally marks. (Place one tally mark for each spoonful of an ingredient you used.) Use words to describe the color, texture, and crystals of each rock.

Igneous Rock Chart

Rocks	Materials Mixed Together						Results		
	Plaster	Water	Vermiculite	Sand	Black Paint		Color	Texture (e.g, smooth, rough)	Can you see any crystal pieces?
Rock #1									
Rock #2									
Rock #3									
Rock #4									

Integrating Science with Reading Instruction · 3–4 © 2002 Creative Teaching Press

Name _____ Date _____

Volcanoes

Why do volcanoes make several types of igneous rocks?

Results and Conclusions

1 If you had real igneous rocks to observe, describe some ways they were alike.

_____

How were they different?

_____

2 Did any of your rocks look the same? _____ Which ones?

_____

How were they the same?

_____

3 Did any of your rocks look different from each other? _____ Which ones?

_____

How were they different?

_____

4 Which rock was your favorite? _____

Why?

_____

5 Why do volcanoes make several types of igneous rocks?

_____

Integrating Science with Reading Instruction · 3–4 © 2002 Creative Teaching Press

Catch a Clue

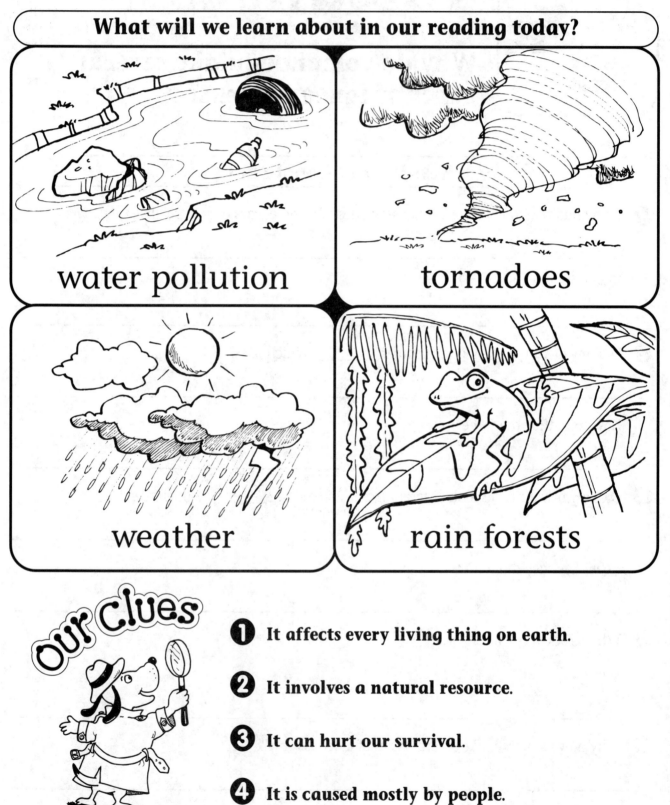

What will we learn about in our reading today?

water pollution

tornadoes

weather

rain forests

Our Clues

1 It affects every living thing on earth.

2 It involves a natural resource.

3 It can hurt our survival.

4 It is caused mostly by people.

Integrating Science with Reading Instruction · 3–4 © 2002 Creative Teaching Press

Concept Map

Facts we already know about **water pollution,** and the new facts we have learned

Water Pollution

Word Warm-Up

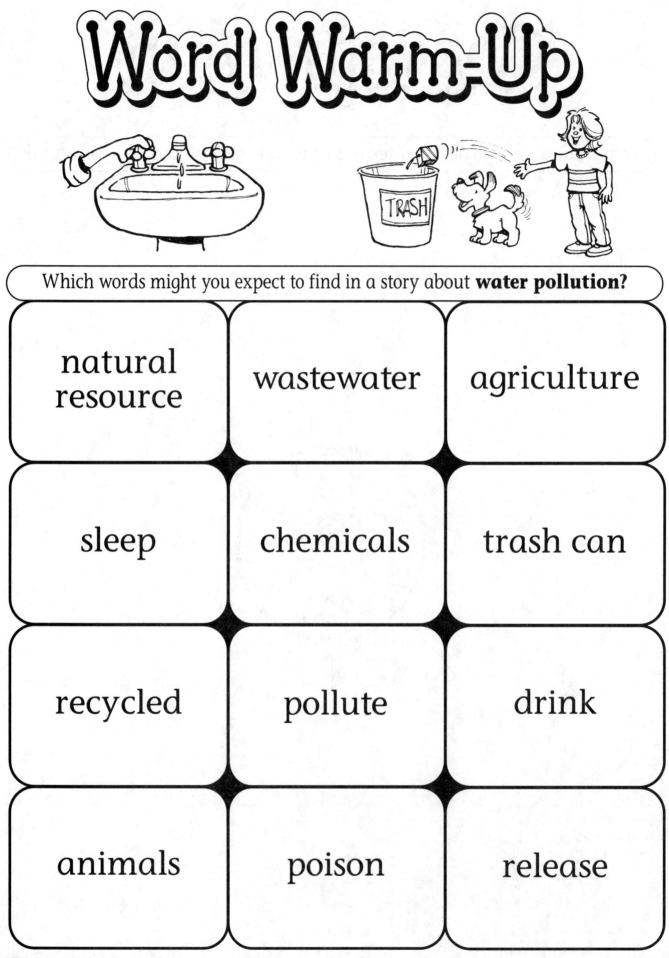

Which words might you expect to find in a story about **water pollution?**

natural resource	wastewater	agriculture
sleep	chemicals	trash can
recycled	pollute	drink
animals	poison	release

Integrating Science with Reading Instruction • 3–4 © 2002 Creative Teaching Press

Water Pollution

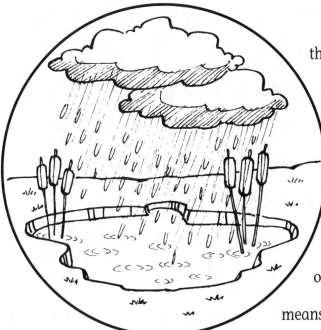

Of all the things you need to live, what is one of the most important? That is right! Water. Believe it or not, people can live for weeks without food. People can only live for a few days without water. Water is one of our most critical natural resources.

We need to take care of the water in our oceans and rivers because it is all recycled. This means it is used over and over again. Have you brought your lunch to school in a paper bag that had already been used? If you spilled milk on it and then squashed it in the mud, would you want to use that same bag again the next day? This is similar to what happens to the water we use. If we do not take care of our water, it will be ruined like that dirty lunch bag.

Many things can pollute the water in our oceans and rivers. One cause of water pollution is wastewater. Wastewater is the water left over after we do laundry, flush the toilet, or use the sink. It runs in the street, then into storm drains, and into the ocean. Luckily, most of the water that goes down the drains inside our homes goes through a water treatment plant. At the water treatment plant, this wastewater is cleaned with special chemicals and released. This water is reused to water parks and golf courses, or it is put back into the rivers and oceans. This water is not used for drinking and cooking.

Another example of water pollution is an oil spill. This is when oil tankers accidentally spill oil in the ocean. Thousands of fish, birds, and other animals are harmed or killed when there is an

Integrating Science with Reading Instruction · 3–4 © 2002 Creative Teaching Press

oil spill. Can you imagine having petroleum oil poured all over your food? Would you want to eat it? What if you did eat your food with petroleum oil on it? Do you think it would be safe? After an oil spill, animals are harmed or die because they cannot breathe. Sometimes they get poisoned because the food they eat has oil on it. Or, their food dies and they do not have enough to eat.

Another way our water gets polluted is from chemicals. This can happen in agriculture. Sometimes too many chemicals are used when we grow food, raise livestock, or prepare foods to be sold. The extra chemicals can flow into rivers or streams and pollute them. This harms the plants and animals that live in the water.

What can you do to help keep our water clean? The easiest thing you can do is to throw your trash in a trash can and not on the street. Trash on the street could end up in our rivers or oceans through a storm drain. You can save water in your home or at school. This helps because less water will go down the drain and become wastewater. To save water, turn off the water while you brush your teeth. You can also take a short shower and ask your parents to only run the dishwasher when they have a full load. There are also special ways to throw away paints, aerosol cans, litter, pet waste, and things made of plastic. Remember to help keep our water clean so you always have a glass of refreshing clean water to drink when you need it!

Integrating Science with Reading Instruction · 3–4 © 2002 Creative Teaching Press

Comprehension Questions

Literal Questions

1 What are three examples of water pollution?

2 What is the easiest thing you can do to keep our water clean?

3 What is a water treatment plant?

4 Why is it harmful to throw trash down storm drains?

5 What are some ways we use reused water?

Inferential Questions

1 Why is water important?

2 What effect do you think water pollution has on life cycles and food chains?

3 How does water get recycled in the environment?

4 Why are oil spills so hazardous?

5 Which places at your school could you check to see if water is being wasted?

Making Connections

1 What sources of water did you use today? How did you help conserve water?

2 Name three ways that you can help improve the water pollution problem.

3 What does your school do to prevent polluting the water system?

4 Can you think of any other types of water pollution that have happened and/or ways to prevent water pollution?

Integrating Science with Reading Instruction · 3–4 © 2002 Creative Teaching Press

Name _____   Date _____

Sharpen Your Skills

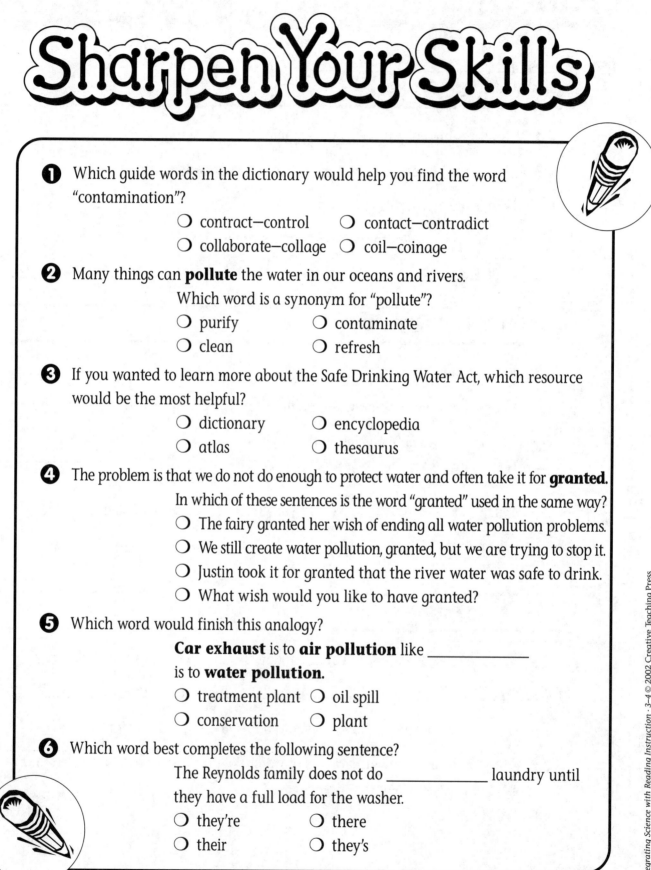

1 Which guide words in the dictionary would help you find the word "contamination"?

○ contract–control   ○ contact–contradict
○ collaborate–collage ○ coil–coinage

2 Many things can **pollute** the water in our oceans and rivers.
Which word is a synonym for "pollute"?

○ purify   ○ contaminate
○ clean   ○ refresh

3 If you wanted to learn more about the Safe Drinking Water Act, which resource would be the most helpful?

○ dictionary   ○ encyclopedia
○ atlas   ○ thesaurus

4 The problem is that we do not do enough to protect water and often take it for **granted.**
In which of these sentences is the word "granted" used in the same way?

○ The fairy granted her wish of ending all water pollution problems.
○ We still create water pollution, granted, but we are trying to stop it.
○ Justin took it for granted that the river water was safe to drink.
○ What wish would you like to have granted?

5 Which word would finish this analogy?

Car exhaust is to **air pollution** like _____
is to **water pollution.**

○ treatment plant ○ oil spill
○ conservation   ○ plant

6 Which word best completes the following sentence?

The Reynolds family does not do _____ laundry until they have a full load for the washer.

○ they're   ○ there
○ their   ○ they's

Integrating Science with Reading Instruction · 3–4 © 2002 Creative Teaching Press

Name _____   Date _____

Get Logical

Paul, Marla, Carlotta, and Trenton are each trying to help minimize water pollution. Use the clues below to decide what each student is doing to help the environment.

Clues

1 Carlotta makes a difference at least twice a day.

2 Trenton helps his mom once a week with this chore. They save water.

3 When Paul is finished, he takes the plastic materials to a special place.

4 Marla makes a difference every day.

	Paul	Marla	Carlotta	Trenton
Takes a shorter shower				
Turns off the water while brushing teeth				
Sorts trash for recycling				
Washes full loads of laundry				

Paul _____.

Marla _____.

Carlotta _____.

Trenton _____.

Water Pollution

What are some ways to remove pollution from water?

Teacher Background Information

Water pollution comes from many sources and often cannot be detected with the naked eye. Water that looks pretty clean can still be polluted. In addition to the more obvious types of pollution (e.g., trash, spilled oil, cast-off junk from society), chemicals from rain runoff, factories, or agriculture can also pollute the water of lakes, rivers, and oceans in more subtle ways. Many chemicals interact with the dissolved oxygen in the water (both fresh and ocean) and reduce the oxygen available for aquatic and marine life. Scientists test water samples to detect and monitor various types of pollution. If the water is not safe, signs will be posted warning the public not to drink, swim, or go boating in that particular area for the time being. The water will be tested again and the public notified when it is safe again.

Experiment Results

Students should discover that it is easiest to remove street trash and dirt, as you can see the pieces. Some can be removed with the spoon and the rest by filtering with the strainer and paper towel. The "oil spill" can be partly removed with the spoon or by filtering but not completely. They should observe droplets of oil still on the water's surface even after filtering. The "agricultural chemicals" (food coloring) are the hardest to remove because the chemicals are dissolved in the water and you cannot see any pieces. In real life, the chemicals are often colorless and cannot be detected with the naked eye. Students may come up with a variety of other suggestions as ways to remove pollutants from water. No matter what they suggest, they will gain an understanding that it is not always easy to clean up polluted water.

Integrating Science with Reading Instruction · 3–4 © 2002 Creative Teaching Press

Water Pollution

What are some ways to remove pollution from water?

Procedure

1 Fill 3 cups one-half full of water.

2 Add 1 drop of food coloring to the first cup. Stir with the plastic spoon. (The food coloring represents agricultural chemicals that can pollute the water.)

3 Use the hole punch to punch 10–15 little bits of paper. Add these and a spoonful of soil to the second cup. Stir with the spoon. (This represents street trash and dirt.)

4 Add 2 spoonfuls of vegetable oil to the third cup. Stir with the spoon. (This represents an oil spill.)

5 Use the plastic spoon, the strainer, and a paper towel to try to remove the "pollution" from one cup. Using the same cup, place a paper towel inside the strainer. Pour the contents of the cup through the strainer into the small bowl. Observe the water that is collected in the bowl under the strainer to see if the "pollution" was removed.

6 Repeat step 5 using the other two cups with "polluted" water samples.

MATERIALS

(per group)
- ✔ 3 plastic cups
- ✔ water
- ✔ food coloring
- ✔ plastic spoon
- ✔ hole punch
- ✔ paper
- ✔ soil
- ✔ vegetable oil
- ✔ small strainer
- ✔ paper towels
- ✔ small bowl

Integrating Science with Reading Instruction · 3–4 © 2002 Creative Teaching Press

Water Pollution

What are some ways to remove pollution from water?

Results and Conclusions

1 Were you able to remove any of the "agricultural chemicals" (food coloring) from the water using the spoon or by straining the water? _____ Why or why not?

_____

2 Were you able to remove any of the "street trash" and dirt using the spoon or by straining the water? _____ Why or why not?

_____

3 Were you able to remove any of the "oil spill" using the spoon or by straining the water? _____ Why or why not?

_____

4 Which type of water pollution was the easiest to clean up?

_____

5 Which type of water pollution do you think is the hardest to clean up?

_____

6 If the "agricultural chemicals" did not color the water, would you be able to tell if the water was polluted?

_____

7 What are some ways that pollutants can be removed from water?

_____

Can you think of any other ways that might work?

_____

Integrating Science with Reading Instruction · 3–4 © 2002 Creative Teaching Press

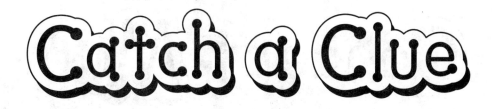

Catch a Clue

Integrating Science with Reading Instruction · 3–4 © 2002 Creative Teaching Press

What will we learn about in our reading today?

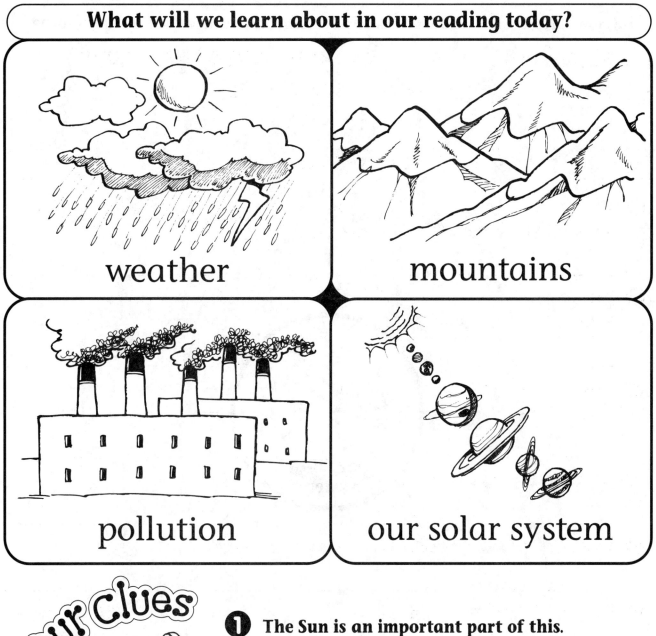

weather

mountains

pollution

our solar system

Our Clues

1 The Sun is an important part of this.

2 It affects our day and night.

3 The parts of this are made out of rocks or gases.

4 Astronomers study this.

Concept Map

Facts we already know about **our solar system,** and the new facts we have learned

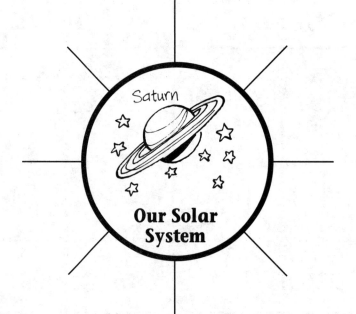

Integrating Science with Reading Instruction · 3–4 © 2002 Creative Teaching Press

Word Warm-Up

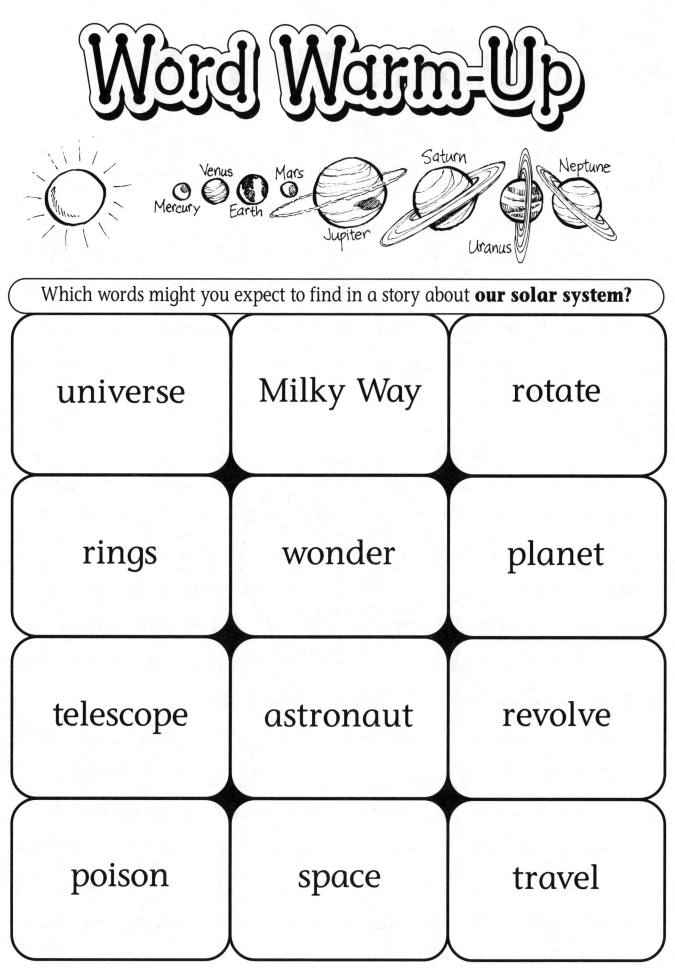

Mercury Venus Earth Mars Jupiter Saturn Uranus Neptune

Which words might you expect to find in a story about **our solar system?**

universe	Milky Way	rotate
rings	wonder	planet
telescope	astronaut	revolve
poison	space	travel

Integrating Science with Reading Instruction · 3–4 © 2002 Creative Teaching Press

Our Solar System

Do you ever dream of going into space to see the wonders of the universe? You really already travel in space. Our spaceship is the planet Earth. It travels at the speed of 67,000 miles (107, 200 km) an hour!

Our solar system is in a small area of outer space called the Milky Way Galaxy. Our solar system is made up of our planet Earth, the Sun, seven other planets, dwarf planets, many moons, and other space objects. The planets that make up our solar system are made of rock or gases. Earth, Mercury, Venus, and Mars are all made of rock. Saturn, Jupiter, Uranus, and Neptune are made of different gases. They have rings of ice, dust, and rock around them. On August 24, 2006, Pluto was redefined as a dwarf planet.

The Sun is a large star at the center of our solar system. It is made up of hot gases. All things in our solar system move around the Sun. One full path around the Sun is called a revolution. As the planets move around the Sun, they also turn around in circles, or rotate. The time it takes a planet to turn around one time in a circle is called a "day." To see how a planet rotates, stand up and look at one spot on the wall. Then, slowly turn your body around until you are looking at that same spot again. Now, do this again, but carefully walk around your desk as you are turning around. You just made one revolution while you were rotating! It is not an easy thing to do, is it?

If you look at all of the planets in a row starting with the one closest to the Sun, you would see Mercury, Venus, Earth, Mars, Jupiter, Saturn, Uranus, and Neptune. Mercury is a bit larger than our moon. Dust, rocks, and bowl-shaped holes called craters cover it. Thick poisonous clouds surround Venus. Earth is the only planet in our solar system that is known to sustain life. Mars is called the "Red Planet." Jupiter is the largest planet in our solar system. Did you know you could fit 318 planet Earths inside of Jupiter? Saturn is almost as large as Jupiter. Saturn is best known for its band

Integrating Science with Reading Instruction · 3–4 © 2002 Creative Teaching Press

of rings. Did you know that a day on Saturn is only $10\frac{1}{2}$ hours long? That means if you lived on Saturn, your school day would be much shorter! It would get dark after only 5 hours! Uranus and Neptune are both very cold planets. This is because they are so far away from the Sun. Uranus rotates in a different way than the other planets. It rotates on its side instead of upright.

The best way to watch our solar system is through a telescope at night. A telescope helps you see things millions of miles away. Would you like to fly into outer space? Then, maybe you would like to be an astronaut. Can you imagine what it would be like to visit another planet up close? Which one would you choose? Or, maybe you would rather be an astronomer and study outer space from here on Earth.

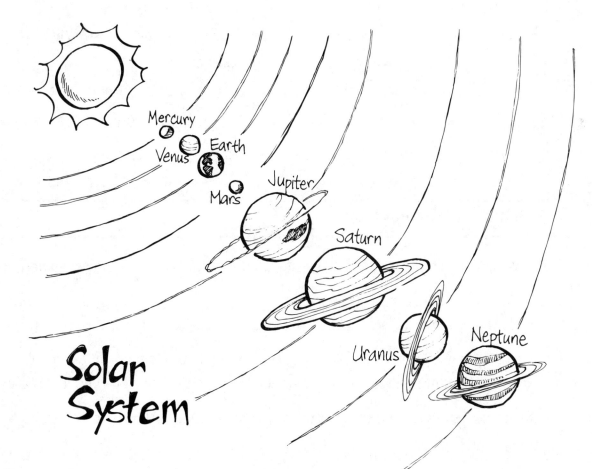

Comprehension Questions

? Literal Questions

1 What is the order of the planets, starting from the Sun?

2 What makes up our solar system?

3 Which planet is best known for its colorful rings of ice, dust, and rock?

4 Which planet is known as the "Red Planet"?

5 How can you observe our solar system?

? Inferential Questions

1 "Solar" comes from the word "sol," which means "sun." How do you think the term "solar system" was created? Why?

2 Which planet do you predict is the hottest and which is the coolest? Why?

3 Many astronomers dream of being able to travel to a distant planet one day. Do you think people could ever live on Venus in the future? Why or why not?

4 After reading about the different planets, which seems most like our Earth? Why?

5 What subjects do you think astronomers need to study to learn about the stars and planets?

? Making Connections

1 Which planet would you like to visit the most? Why? What would you expect to see there?

2 Do you believe that there are people living on any other planets? Why or why not?

3 In 2001, a man paid the Russian government millions of dollars for a ride into space. What are the pros and cons of allowing people to pay for rides into space?

4 Does this story remind you of any books you have read? Which ones? Why?

Integrating Science with Reading Instruction · 3–4 © 2002 Creative Teaching Press

Name _____   Date _____

Sharpen Your Skills

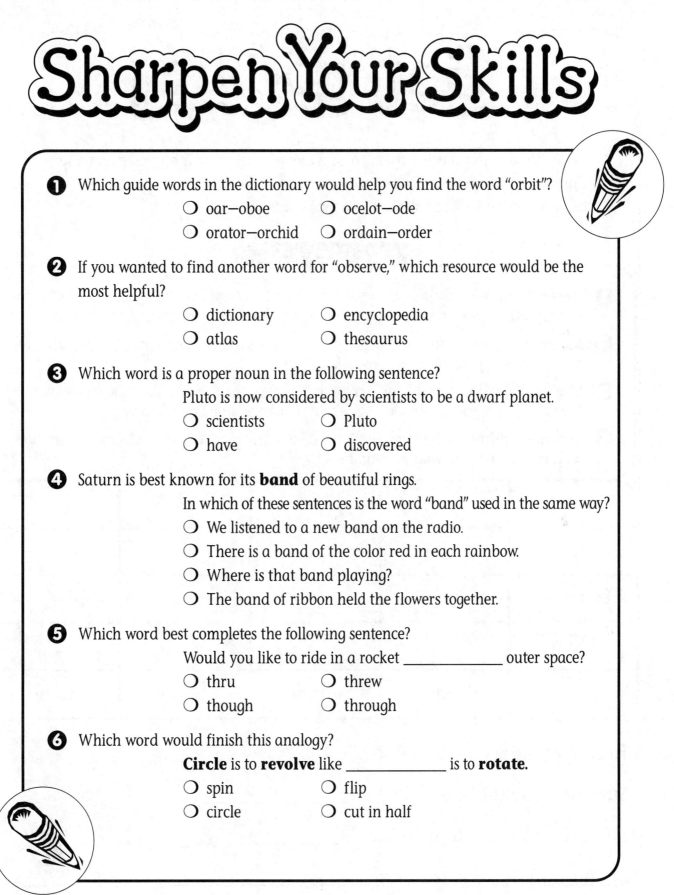

1 Which guide words in the dictionary would help you find the word "orbit"?
- ○ oar–oboe
- ○ ocelot–ode
- ○ orator–orchid
- ○ ordain–order

2 If you wanted to find another word for "observe," which resource would be the most helpful?
- ○ dictionary
- ○ encyclopedia
- ○ atlas
- ○ thesaurus

3 Which word is a proper noun in the following sentence?

Pluto is now considered by scientists to be a dwarf planet.
- ○ scientists
- ○ Pluto
- ○ have
- ○ discovered

4 Saturn is best known for its **band** of beautiful rings.

In which of these sentences is the word "band" used in the same way?
- ○ We listened to a new band on the radio.
- ○ There is a band of the color red in each rainbow.
- ○ Where is that band playing?
- ○ The band of ribbon held the flowers together.

5 Which word best completes the following sentence?

Would you like to ride in a rocket _____ outer space?
- ○ thru
- ○ threw
- ○ though
- ○ through

6 Which word would finish this analogy?

Circle is to **revolve** like _____ is to **rotate.**
- ○ spin
- ○ flip
- ○ circle
- ○ cut in half

Integrating Science with Reading Instruction · 3–4 © 2002 Creative Teaching Press

Name _____   Date _____

Get Logical

In Mr. Wilson's class, each student chose a planet to travel to if he or she had a special rocket. Each student wrote a riddle about his or her chosen planet. Use the clues below to decide which planet each student wanted to visit.

Clues

1 **Hector's riddle** I am the first planet from the Sun. I am very hot. I am named after the Roman god of travel in mythology because I move quickly across the sky.

2 **Summer's riddle** I am a dwarf planet. My name is the same as a popular character from an amusement park. I am made of rock and ice.

3 **Sharon's riddle** I am the same color as a color in the rainbow. I am the fourth planet from the Sun. A day on my planet is about as long as a day on Earth.

4 **Shana's riddle** People think that I am a beautiful planet. I am made up of gases, not rock. I have a band of rings around me.

	Hector	Summer	Sharon	Shana
Saturn				
Mars				
Mercury				
Pluto				

Hector would like to travel to _____.

Summer would like to travel to _____.

Sharon would like to travel to _____.

Shana would like to travel to _____.

Mercury
Venus
Earth

Integrating Science with Reading Instruction · 3–4 © 2002 Creative Teaching Press

Our Solar System

What keeps the planets in orbit as they revolve around the Sun?

Teacher Background Information

There are two forces at work that keep the planets in orbit around the Sun. The first is inertia, which is the tendency of a body in motion to stay in motion unless acted upon by some other force. Likewise, a body at rest will stay at rest unless some force moves it. This is Newton's first law of motion. Simply put, if you are running forward quickly, you cannot stop instantly. It takes a few moments to slow down and stop. Since the planets are moving, they will tend to keep moving unless something else stops them. The planets would normally want to move forward in a straight line. However, this is where the second force comes in to play. It is gravity. Gravity is the natural attraction between objects. The bigger and heavier the object, the greater its pull of gravity. The Earth's gravity pulls down on everything and everybody. This is what keeps the Earth together and prevents us from flying off into outer space. The Sun is so much bigger than any of the planets, that its gravitational pull prevents the planets from "flying off" into space. Fortunately, there is a balance between these two forces. The Sun's gravity is not strong enough to pull the planets down into it. The planets' inertia is not strong enough for them to fly off into space. Thus, the planets stay in orbit around the Sun.

Experiment Results

Students should observe that it is hard to hold the book up in their outstretched hand, as gravity is pulling down on the book and their arm. The tennis ball falls to the floor and bounces. Gravity is pulling on the tennis ball, too. Everything is being pulled down toward the Earth. When they try to roll the ball across the table, it is difficult to make it stop. Usually, it will continue to roll and fall off the table. The inertia keeps the moving ball in motion. When students release the string attached to the eraser, the eraser flies off in a different direction, away from them. Their hand has to keep pulling on the string to keep the eraser in orbit around them. This is what the Sun's gravity does to the planets. The two forces of gravity and inertia keep the planets in orbit around the Sun.

Integrating Science with Reading Instruction · 3–4 © 2002 Creative Teaching Press

Our Solar System

What keeps the planets in orbit as they revolve around the Sun?

Procedure

1 Stretch out your arm, and hold the book in your hand. Wait for 1 minute. Observe how it feels and whether it is easy or hard to maintain your position.

2 Hold a tennis ball in your outstretched hand. Let go of it. Observe what happens.

3 Gently roll the tennis ball across the table. Try to roll the ball quickly, but have it stop before it falls off the table. Observe what happens.

4 Tie the piece of string around the chalkboard eraser.

5 Stand in an open area outside away from others, and carefully whirl the eraser around your head two to three times. Let go of the string suddenly, and observe what happens.

6 Whirl the eraser around your head again four to six times. Observe what your hand is doing as the eraser moves.

MATERIALS

(per group)
- ✔ heavy book
- ✔ tennis ball
- ✔ 3' (1 m) piece of string
- ✔ chalkboard eraser

Integrating Science with Reading Instruction · 3–4 © 2002 Creative Teaching Press

Our Solar System

What keeps the planets in orbit as they revolve around the Sun?

Results and Conclusions

1 How did you feel after holding up the heavy book for 1 minute? _____ Was it easy or hard to maintain your position? _____ Why?

_____

2 Were you able to roll the tennis ball across the table quickly without it falling off? _____ Why or why not?

_____

3 What do you call the force that keeps the ball moving forward?

_____

4 What force do you think was acting on the book, your hand, and the tennis ball? _____ In which direction did everything want to go?

_____

5 What happened when you let go of the string attached to the eraser? _____ In which direction did the eraser go?

_____

6 When you whirled the eraser again, what did your hand do to keep the eraser "in orbit"?

_____

7 What keeps the planets in orbit as they revolve around the Sun?

_____

Catch a Clue

What will we learn about in our reading today?

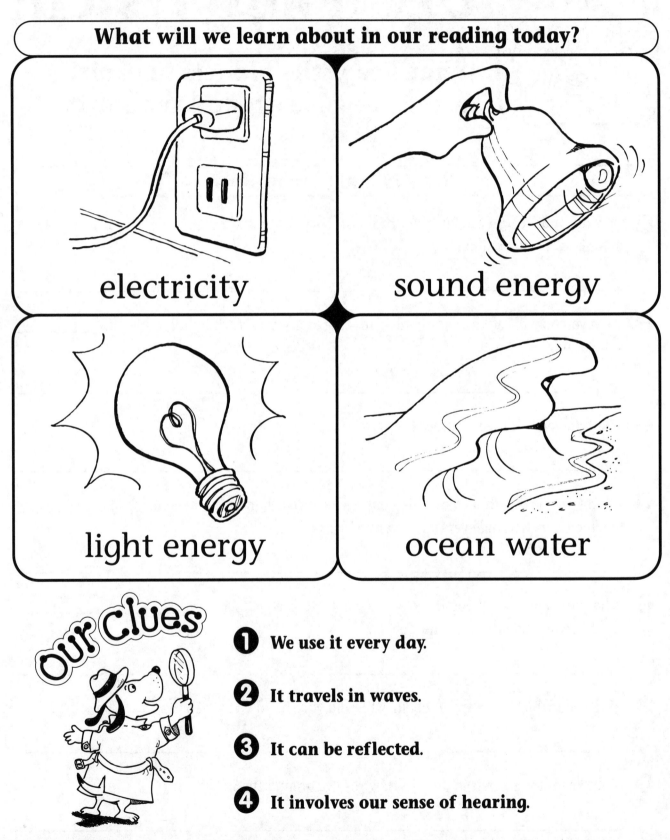

electricity

sound energy

light energy

ocean water

Our Clues

1. We use it every day.

2. It travels in waves.

3. It can be reflected.

4. It involves our sense of hearing.

Integrating Science with Reading Instruction · 3–4 © 2002 Creative Teaching Press

Concept Map

Facts we already know about **sound energy,** and the new facts we have learned

Word Warm-Up

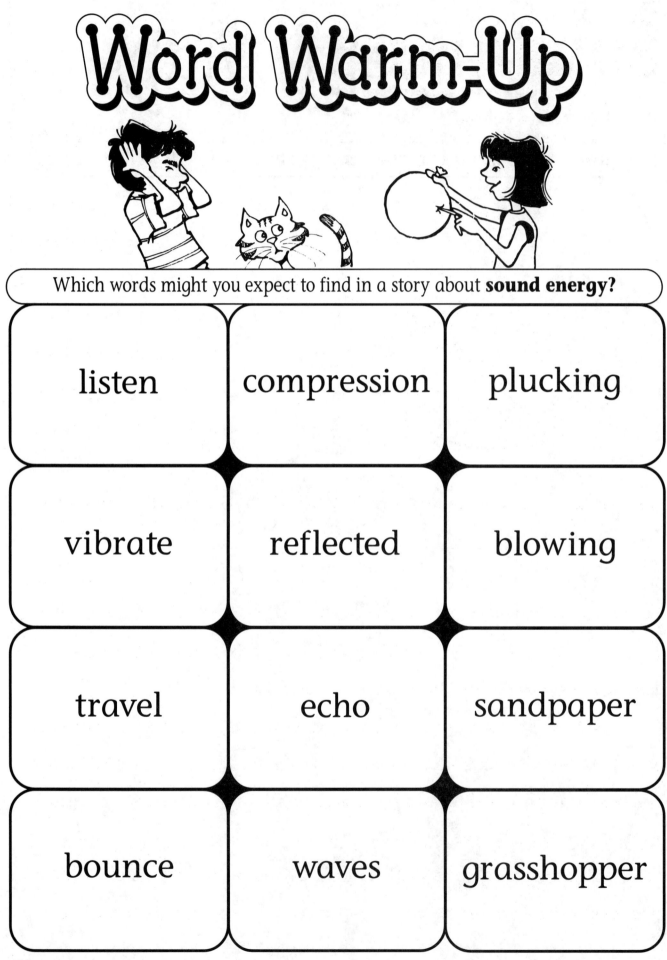

Which words might you expect to find in a story about **sound energy?**

listen	compression	plucking
vibrate	reflected	blowing
travel	echo	sandpaper
bounce	waves	grasshopper

Integrating Science with Reading Instruction · 3–4 © 2002 Creative Teaching Press

Sound Energy

Sounds are all around us. Each day we hear people talk, dogs bark, the sounds of traffic, or music. The sound of an alarm clock may wake you up to get ready for school. Do you know what sound is? Sound is a form of energy. Sound is made when something causes an object to vibrate. This means the object moves quickly back and forth. These vibrations move through the air until they reach our ears. Our ears and brain interpret these as different kinds of sounds. Sounds can move through solids, liquids, and gases. In fact, sound moves more easily through solids than it does through liquids. It travels a bit slower through gases like the air.

How does sound travel? Sound moves in waves called compression waves. This means that the waves press together. Then, they separate and move from where they began to the place that will get the sound. Have you ever dropped a rock in a calm pool of water? Did you see rings of waves move away from the rock? Sound waves travel in the same way.

Sound can also be reflected by some things. An echo is reflected sound. You hear an echo when the sound waves bounce off of an object. Echoes are mostly heard when you stand in a canyon or a large empty room. The sound will bounce off the sides of the canyon or the walls of the room.

How can you make a sound? There are four main ways to make a sound. They are striking, stroking, plucking, and blowing. Striking is just hitting an object, or a part of it, against something. This will make the object begin vibrating. A child banging a spoon on the table and a musical instrument, such as a drum or cymbals, both make sounds by striking.

Stroking is a form of rubbing. One object is rubbed with another object. If you rub sandpaper over a piece of wood, you will make sound from stroking. A grasshopper rubs its wing across little ridges on its back leg to make sounds. Crickets rub both of their wings together to make sound.

Plucking is a picking action with the fingers that makes the object vibrate. To make sound by plucking, you can pluck a rubber band, the strings of a banjo, or a guitar.

Blowing is another way to make sounds. When we talk, we blow air over our vocal cords. This makes them vibrate. Put your hand on your throat and say something. Can you feel your vocal cords vibrating? You can make sounds by blowing over the opening of a jar, through a whistle, or into a flute. The croak of a frog and the chirp of a bird are both sounds made by blowing.

Listen to the world around you. You will hear many different sounds. See if you can tell how each sound is made. Also, think about what is happening to make the sounds you hear.

Integrating Science with Reading Instruction · 3–4 © 2002 Creative Teaching Press

Comprehension Questions

? Literal Questions

1. What are some sounds people hear each day?

2. Does sound travel faster through solids, liquids, or gases?

3. What are the four different ways of making sound?

4. What does it mean when something vibrates?

5. Explain how sound travels in waves.

? Inferential Questions

1. Do you think sound can travel through outer space? Why or why not?

2. What makes earplugs work?

3. Compare and contrast how a cricket, grasshopper, dog, and person make sounds.

4. Why do you think loud noises are harmful to our ears?

5. Why doesn't every living creature just talk to communicate?

? Making Connections

1. Listen carefully. What sounds can you hear? Where is the sound originating from? Can you tell if the sound is made from striking, stroking, plucking, or blowing?

2. How high do you turn up the volume on your radio? Is it a safe volume for your ears?

3. Can you whistle? How is sound made when you whistle?

4. What sounds relate to personal safety at home, on the road, and at your school?

Integrating Science with Reading Instruction · 3–4 © 2002 Creative Teaching Press

Name _____   Date _____

Sharpen Your Skills

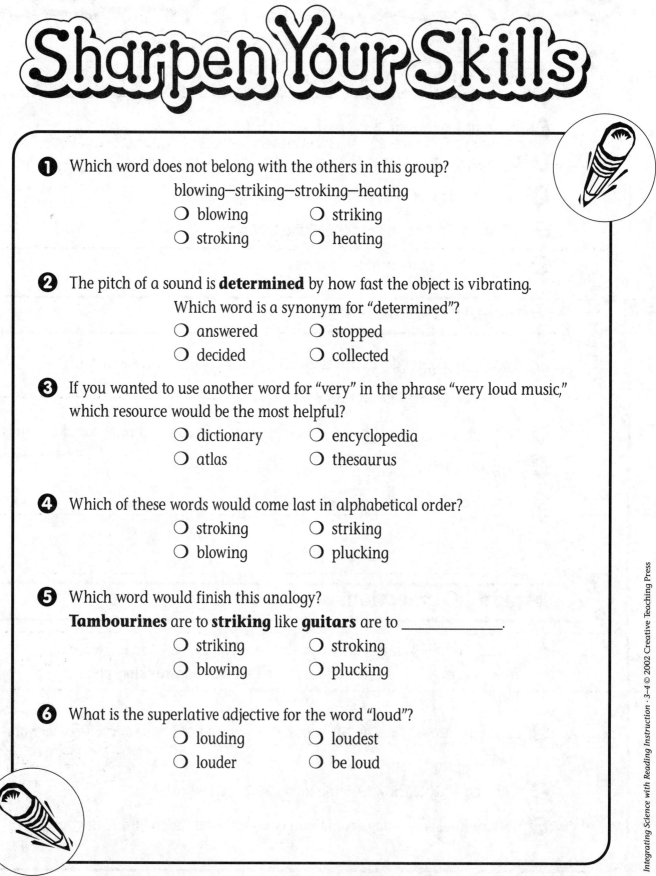

1 Which word does not belong with the others in this group?

blowing–striking–stroking–heating

- ○ blowing
- ○ striking
- ○ stroking
- ○ heating

2 The pitch of a sound is **determined** by how fast the object is vibrating.

Which word is a synonym for "determined"?

- ○ answered
- ○ stopped
- ○ decided
- ○ collected

3 If you wanted to use another word for "very" in the phrase "very loud music," which resource would be the most helpful?

- ○ dictionary
- ○ encyclopedia
- ○ atlas
- ○ thesaurus

4 Which of these words would come last in alphabetical order?

- ○ stroking
- ○ striking
- ○ blowing
- ○ plucking

5 Which word would finish this analogy?

Tambourines are to **striking** like **guitars** are to _____.

- ○ striking
- ○ stroking
- ○ blowing
- ○ plucking

6 What is the superlative adjective for the word "loud"?

- ○ louding
- ○ loudest
- ○ louder
- ○ be loud

Integrating Science with Reading Instruction · 3–4 © 2002 Creative Teaching Press

Name _____   Date _____

Get Logical

The Boogie Woogie Band has four members named Jackson, Eli, Jasmine, and Dana. Use the clues below to decide which instrument each member of the band plays.

Clues

1 Jasmine does not strike or stroke her instrument.

2 Eli makes beautiful music by blowing into his instrument.

3 Dana strikes her instrument very quickly.

4 Jackson rubs his instrument together to make an unusual sound.

	Jackson	Eli	Jasmine	Dana
Drums				
Guitar				
Flute				
Sand Blocks				

Jackson plays the _____.

Eli plays the _____.

Jasmine plays the _____.

Dana plays the _____.

Integrating Science with Reading Instruction · 3–4 © 2002 Creative Teaching Press

Sound Energy

How are different sounds created?

Teacher Background Information

Sound is produced whenever an object vibrates. Vibrations are just the rapid back-and-forth movements of the object. Sometimes the whole object will vibrate. Other times just a part of the object may vibrate and produce a sound. Many ordinary objects can be used to illustrate the four ways of producing sound (i.e., striking, stroking, plucking, and blowing). The faster the object vibrates, the higher the pitch of the sound. Pitch describes how high or low a sound or note is. This is sometimes also referred to as the frequency of the sound. The human ear cannot hear every single frequency. Smaller, thinner objects can vibrate faster than larger, fatter objects. That is because there is less matter in the object that has to vibrate back and forth. The strength of the vibrations determines the sound's volume or intensity. Volume describes how loud or soft a sound is.

Many musical instruments use a cone-shaped structure to amplify the sound and create a louder volume. These cone-shaped instruments work like a megaphone. The flared end of a clarinet, a trumpet, or a tuba helps to create a louder sound. Other musical instruments have a "sound box" that produces a louder sound. The body or case of a violin or cello helps to create louder sounds. In advance, put the materials for each group in a separate resealable plastic bag.

Experiment Results

All of the objects in the "sound bag" except the rubber band can make a sound by striking. Students will most likely mention the craft sticks, the bell, and the comb. They can rub the craft sticks or the straws together to produce stroking sounds. They can pick at the teeth of the comb or pluck the rubber band to produce plucking sounds. They can blow across the tops of the straw pieces to create sounds. (Make sure students do not insert the straw pieces into their mouth.) The following are examples of musical instruments that create sounds using the four different movements: striking (drum and xylophone), stroking (violin and cello), plucking (harp and violin), and blowing (trumpet and tuba).

Integrating Science with Reading Instruction · 3–4 © 2002 Creative Teaching Press

Sound Energy

How are different sounds created?

Procedure

1 Remove all the objects from your "sound bag."

2 Manipulate the objects in different ways to try to create sounds. Do not put the straw pieces in your mouth.

3 Try to strike, stroke, pluck, and blow on each object to see which works the best, and think about what is vibrating to create the sound you are making.

4 Discuss with your group some other examples of musical instruments that make sounds in each of these four ways.

MATERIALS

(per group)
- ✔ 2 craft sticks
- ✔ comb
- ✔ rubber band
- ✔ bell
- ✔ short piece of a straw
- ✔ longer piece of a straw

Integrating Science with Reading Instruction · 3–4 © 2002 Creative Teaching Press

Name _____ Date _____

Sound Energy

How are different sounds created?

Results and Conclusions

1 Which object(s) in the bag can make a sound by striking?

_____

2 Which object(s) in the bag can make a sound by stroking?

_____

3 Which object(s) in the bag can make a sound by plucking?

_____

4 Which object(s) in the bag can make a sound by blowing?

_____

5 Which instrument would play higher notes (have a higher pitch), the violin or the cello?

_____

Why?

_____

6 How are different sounds created?

_____

Integrating Science with Reading Instruction · 3–4 © 2002 Creative Teaching Press

Catch a Clue

What will we learn about in our reading today?

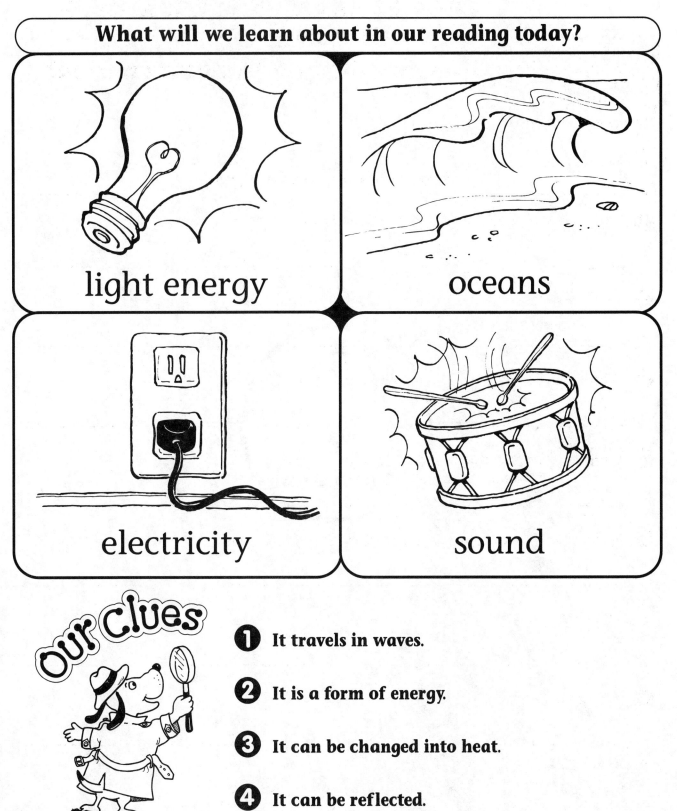

light energy

oceans

electricity

sound

Our Clues

1. It travels in waves.

2. It is a form of energy.

3. It can be changed into heat.

4. It can be reflected.

Concept Map

Facts we already know about **light energy,** and the new facts we have learned

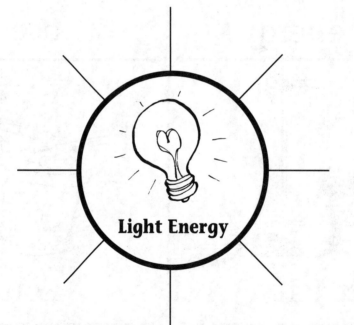

Light Energy

Integrating Science with Reading Instruction ·3–4 © 2002 Creative Teaching Press

Word Warm-Up

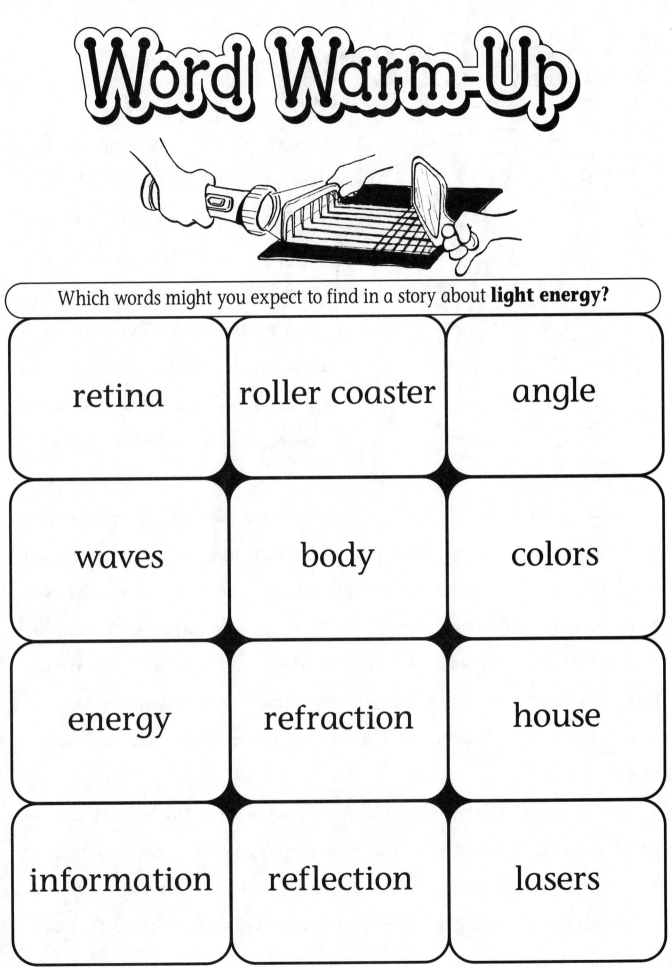

Which words might you expect to find in a story about **light energy?**

retina	roller coaster	angle
waves	body	colors
energy	refraction	house
information	reflection	lasers

Integrating Science with Reading Instruction · 3–4 © 2002 Creative Teaching Press

Light Energy

Light is all over our world. We see light with our eyes. Our eyes use a light-sensitive area called the retina. Light moves in a straight line, but it is not straight like an arrow. Light moves in waves. Think of a fast roller coaster that goes up and down as it moves forward. These roller coaster light waves move forward at 186,000 miles (300,000 km) per second. Now that is fast! Light gives our eyes and brain information about the world around us. But what is light?

Light is a form of energy. It is useful to us. Light comes from things such as flashlights, candles, lamps, fires, and the sun. Although light waves move in a straight line, the light can be bent. This will change its direction. Then, it will move in a straight line in a new way. This happens when light goes through something clear at a slant. Have you seen what happens when you put your feet in a swimming pool? What happens when you place a pencil in a glass of water? Does the object seem bent at the top of the water? It sure does! This is from refraction. Refraction, or the bending of light, happens when light goes from one thing to another. In the pool, the light rays refract, or bend, as they move from air into water.

What happens if light lands on something that is not clear? Some of the light will bounce away from the object. This is called reflection. Reflection happens when light hits an object and bounces off. You see a reflection each time you look in a mirror. You see your reflection! Since most mirrors are flat and not clear, they reflect almost all of the light. The light rays bounce off of the mirror. This is like a

Integrating Science with Reading Instruction · 3–4 © 2002 Creative Teaching Press

ball that bounces back to you when you play handball. If the light rays hit the mirror at an angle, they will bounce off that same way. If the light rays hit the mirror straight on, they will bounce straight back to you. This is true of any flat, smooth surface. But, if the surface of an object is not smooth, it will not reflect light very well. This makes the light rays bounce off in many different ways.

How does light help us to see colors? We see objects when light hits them and reflects back to our eyes. Sunlight, or white light, is made up of all the colors of the rainbow. A red shirt looks red because only the red light is reflected. The dye in the shirt soaks up the other colors. A white shirt looks white because it reflects all the colors of light. A black shirt looks black because it soaks up all the colors. No light is reflected back to your eyes. Light that is soaked up, or absorbed, is changed into heat.

Much progress is being made in the world of light technology. There are new uses of light in our lives. There has been work with light to make lasers, holograms, photographs, and medicine. Laser lights are used in CD players, video discs, computers, and the machines that read bar codes on the products you buy at the store. Doctors now use lasers to operate on human hearts, to remove moles, and even to fix eye problems. Lasers are a strong form of just one color of light energy. We would not have these things if we did not have light and understand how it works.

Comprehension Questions

? Literal Questions

1 What is light? How does it travel? How fast does it travel?

2 How do scientists use light?

3 What is refraction?

4 What is reflection?

5 What happens when light is absorbed by an object?

? Inferential Questions

1 If you want to use the sun to bake some apples in a metal cup outside, what color paper should you wrap around your cup? Why?

2 How do carnival mirrors make you look short and fat or tall and skinny?

3 What does an ice-covered lake do to light—absorb most or very little of it? Why?

4 How do you "see" a shirt that has red and blue stripes?

5 In what other ways do you think laser lights are used to help people?

? Making Connections

1 What color shirt are you wearing today? What color of light is being absorbed by it? What colors are being reflected off of it?

2 Why is light energy important in your life?

3 What light sources are in your room, your house, and your school?

4 How can you make light bend?

Integrating Science with Reading Instruction · 3–4 © 2002 Creative Teaching Press

Name _____   Date _____

Sharpen Your Skills

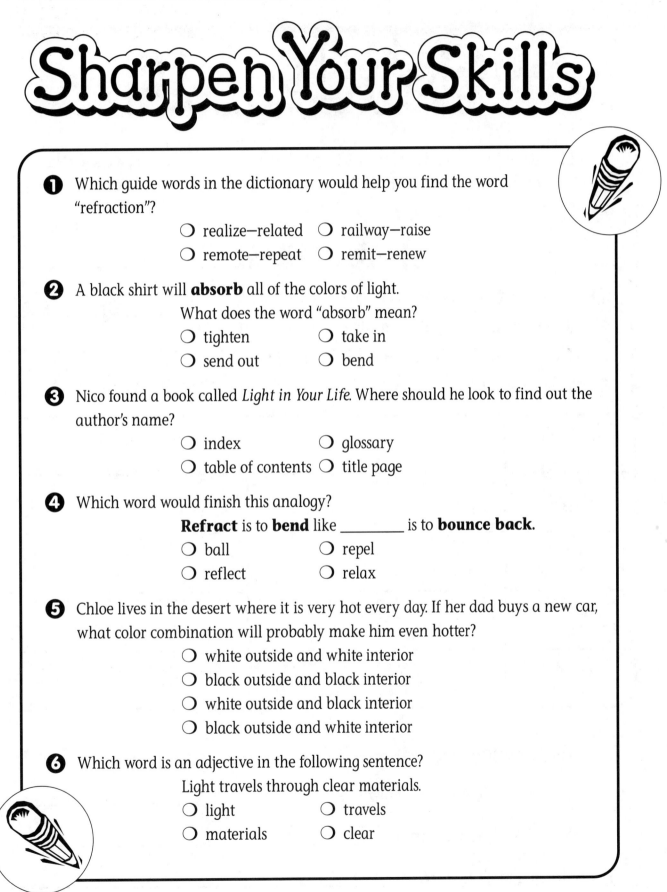

1 Which guide words in the dictionary would help you find the word "refraction"?

- ○ realize–related   ○ railway–raise
- ○ remote–repeat   ○ remit–renew

2 A black shirt will **absorb** all of the colors of light.
What does the word "absorb" mean?

- ○ tighten   ○ take in
- ○ send out   ○ bend

3 Nico found a book called *Light in Your Life*. Where should he look to find out the author's name?

- ○ index   ○ glossary
- ○ table of contents   ○ title page

4 Which word would finish this analogy?
Refract is to **bend** like _____ is to **bounce back**.

- ○ ball   ○ repel
- ○ reflect   ○ relax

5 Chloe lives in the desert where it is very hot every day. If her dad buys a new car, what color combination will probably make him even hotter?

- ○ white outside and white interior
- ○ black outside and black interior
- ○ white outside and black interior
- ○ black outside and white interior

6 Which word is an adjective in the following sentence?
Light travels through clear materials.

- ○ light   ○ travels
- ○ materials   ○ clear

Get Logical

Chloe, Linda, Monica, and Erik each designed an experiment related to light energy. Use the clues below to decide which title best describes each student's experiment.

Clues

1 Monica created an experiment that made light bend.

2 Chloe's experiment involved making light bounce off of objects.

3 Linda's experiment used a prism to create a rainbow.

4 Erik created a hot dog cooker.

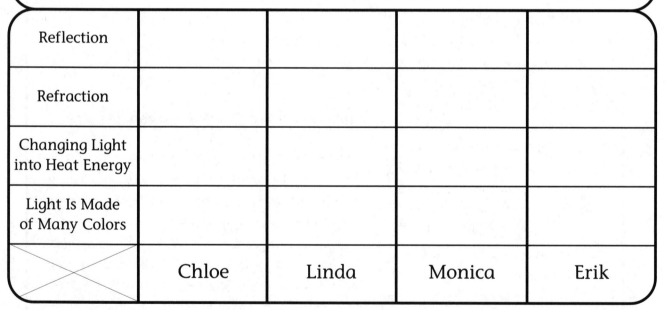

	Chloe	Linda	Monica	Erik
Reflection				
Refraction				
Changing Light into Heat Energy				
Light Is Made of Many Colors				

The title of Chloe's experiment is _____.

The title of Linda's experiment is _____.

The title of Monica's experiment is _____.

The title of Erik's experiment is _____.

Integrating Science with Reading Instruction · 3–4 © 2002 Creative Teaching Press

Light Energy

What is the difference between reflection and refraction of light?

Teacher Background Information

Light energy travels in a wave motion at incredibly high speed until it bumps into something. When light strikes an object, it can do three things: the light can bounce off, pass through it, or be absorbed by it and changed into heat. Most objects reflect some of the light that hits them. When a lot of reflected light from an object reaches our eyes, it makes the object appear shiny. Dull-looking surfaces are not very smooth, and they scatter the light in different directions. The light that passes through an object may pass through directly or it may be bent, or refracted, as it passes through. Transparent objects reflect some of the light that strikes them, but most of the light passes directly through, and we can see clearly what is on the other side. Translucent objects only allow some of the light to pass through. However, this light is refracted and scattered in many directions, so that we cannot see clearly what is on the other side. Opaque objects do not let any light pass through. When light is refracted, the light waves are always bent toward the thicker part of the material it is passing through.

Experiment Results

The overhead transparency has the smoothest surface of the three items in the experiment and should give the best reflection. Materials with a rougher surface scatter the light in different directions and do not give a good reflection. When students look at themselves in the mirror, they will appear to be the same size (although some may not think so). The light was reflected straight back to their eyes. They should be able to see multiple images of themselves looking at themselves when they use the two mirrors. How many images they see depends on how parallel they hold the mirrors. If the mirrors are not upright, they will not be able to see as many repeated images. The light is just being reflected back and forth between the mirrors. Theoretically, they could see an infinite number of images if the mirrors were perfectly parallel. In the experiment with the penny, they should see the penny reappear as the water is slowly added to the pan. The penny did not move. The light was refracted as it passed through the water, making the penny appear to be where it actually was not.

Light Energy

What is the difference between reflection and refraction of light?

Procedure

1 Pick up the overhead transparency, the construction paper, and the waxed paper one at a time. Tilt each material in different directions, and observe if any light is reflected to your eyes. (Does it look shiny?)

2 Feel the surface of each material, and observe any differences.

3 Hold a mirror up in front of your face. Observe your reflection.

4 Now use two mirrors. Hold one in front of your chin, with the "mirror" side facing away from you. Hold the other mirror in your other hand, and extend it out at an arm's length with the mirror side facing you. Try to hold the mirrors upright. (You should be able to see yourself in both mirrors.)

5 Place the penny in the center of the aluminum pan.

6 While looking at the penny, slowly slide your chair backwards until the penny just disappears from view. Remain seated in the same place.

7 Have another group member carefully pour water into the pan. Observe what you see.

8 Empty the water out of the pan, and repeat steps 5–8 until everyone in the group has looked at the penny.

MATERIALS

(per group)
- ✔ overhead transparency
- ✔ piece of construction paper (any color)
- ✔ piece of waxed paper
- ✔ 2–4 mirrors
- ✔ penny (or similar object)
- ✔ small disposable aluminum pan
- ✔ glass of water

Integrating Science with Reading Instruction · 3–4 © 2002 Creative Teaching Press

Name _____   Date _____

Light Energy

What is the difference between reflection and refraction of light?

Results and Conclusions

1 Which material had the smoothest surface—the overhead transparency, the construction paper, or the waxed paper?

_____

2 Which material reflected light the best—the overhead transparency, the construction paper, or the waxed paper? Why?

_____

3 Were you able to see yourself looking at yourself in the two mirrors?

_____

4 How many times could you see yourself? _____

How is this possible?

_____

What is happening to the light?

_____

5 What happened when another group member poured water into the pan that had the penny?

_____

6 Did the penny experiment work because the light was reflected or refracted?

7 What is the difference between reflection and refraction of light?

_____

Integrating Science with Reading Instruction · 3-4 © 2002 Creative Teaching Press

Catch a Clue

What will we learn about in our reading today?

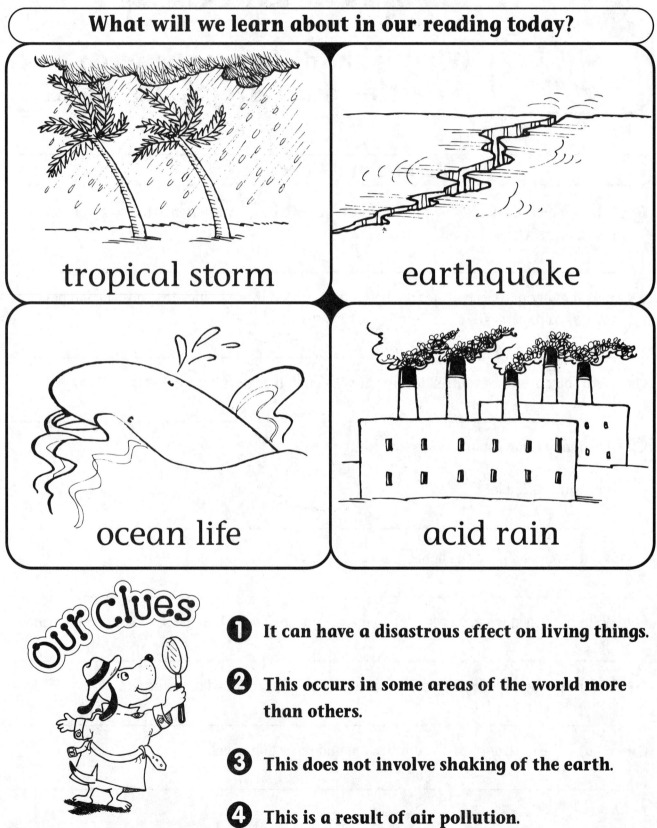

tropical storm

earthquake

ocean life

acid rain

Our Clues

1 It can have a disastrous effect on living things.

2 This occurs in some areas of the world more than others.

3 This does not involve shaking of the earth.

4 This is a result of air pollution.

Integrating Science with Reading Instruction · 3–4 © 2002 Creative Teaching Press

Concept Map

Facts we already know about **acid rain,** and the new facts we have learned

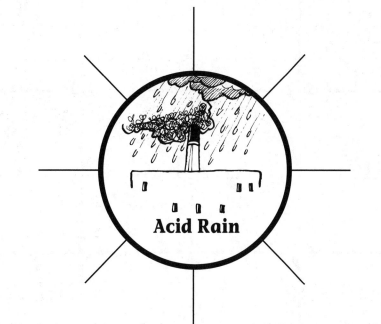

Acid Rain

Integrating Science with Reading Instruction · 3–4 © 2002 Creative Teaching Press

Word Warm-Up

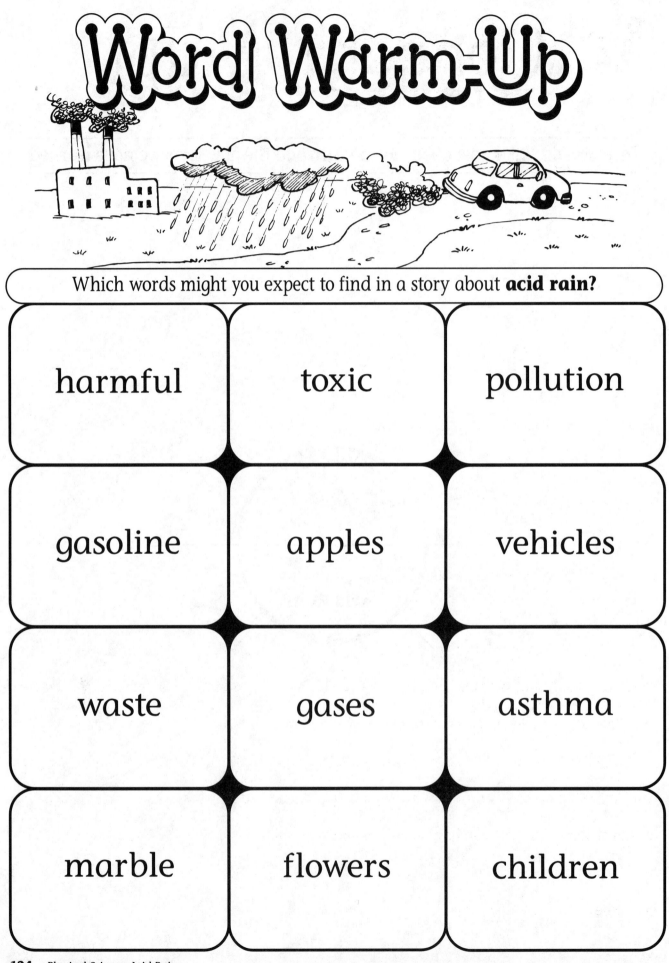

Which words might you expect to find in a story about **acid rain?**

harmful	toxic	pollution
gasoline	apples	vehicles
waste	gases	asthma
marble	flowers	children

Integrating Science with Reading Instruction · 3–4 © 2002 Creative Teaching Press

Acid Rain

We know that rain is important. It helps plants grow, washes off the streets, and makes the air smell fresh. Did you know that there is one kind of rain that is harmful? It is called acid rain.

Acid rain is caused by air pollution. The smoke from cars, buses, and factories combines with small water droplets in the clouds to form an acid. How does this happen? When gasoline and other fuels burn, waste gases are made. Then, they go into the air. These pollutants go up into the clouds. When it rains, the raindrops fall through these polluted clouds. Then, normal rain changes into a weak acid called acid rain. This acid is strong enough to kill trees, dissolve the limestone and marble in buildings, and kill all life in an entire lake. Pretend you are wearing a red shirt. A friend of yours walks by and squirts you with water. But it was not just water. It had bleach in it also! What would the bleach do to your shirt? It would remove some of the color. What would happen if this friend kept squirting your shirt with this bleach water? Soon, your red shirt would have white spots all over it and would be ruined! That is what happens to plants and buildings that get "squirted" with acid rain. After a while, they are not the same either.

There are scientists who measure each rainfall to check if there is acid in it. Some cities have more acid rain than other cities. In many large, crowded cities, there are more vehicles, and the more vehicles there are, the more air pollution there is. Big cities also have more power plants that create air pollution. More air pollution creates more acid rain.

What if you do not live in a crowded area? Can you still see the effects of acid rain? You sure can! Air pollution can be carried by the wind from one area to another. The acid rain can then fall as rain or snow. Acid rain can harm our lakes, fish, trees, and buildings. It can also affect our health. Some health problems that happen because of air pollution and acid rain are asthma, dry coughs, headaches, and a scratchy throat.

Acid rain can dissolve some metals. Some of these metals are poisonous, or toxic. This can cause problems. This toxic metal can dissolve in the water. Some of our fruits, vegetables, and animals take in this polluted water. Then, we may eat these plants or animals for food. This can be harmful to our health.

What can you do to help reduce acid rain? You could walk to school instead of taking the bus or riding in a car. You could also use less energy in your home by always turning off the lights when you are not using them or by not leaving the refrigerator door open when you are not using it. To learn more ways you can help, you could write a letter to a company near you and ask them to tell you about the ways they help control pollution. Anything you do that creates less pollution in the air will help reduce the acid rain problem.

Acid Rain

Integrating Science with Reading Instruction · 3–4 © 2002 Creative Teaching Press

Comprehension Questions

Integrating Science with Reading Instruction · 3–4 © 2002 Creative Teaching Press

? Literal Questions

❶ What is the main cause of acid rain?

❷ How is acid rain related to air pollution?

❸ What are some health problems related to air pollution and acid rain?

❹ What happens when plants absorb acid rain?

❺ What types of areas tend to have more acid rain? Why?

? Inferential Questions

❶ What are pollutants?

❷ Why do you think acid rain affects our health in a negative way?

❸ Why is acid rain harmful to some buildings?

❹ How do you think the food chain is affected by acid rain?

❺ How would walking to school instead of taking the bus or a car help reduce acid rain?

? Making Connections

❶ What can you do to help minimize the air pollution problem?

❷ What kinds of air pollution could be in your neighborhood?

❸ Why is it important for you to help reduce air pollution?

❹ What is the safest way for you to get to school and cause the least amount of air pollution?

Sharpen Your Skills

1 If you put these words in alphabetical order, which word would come right after the word "mercury"?

- ○ marble
- ○ machines
- ○ metal
- ○ toxic

2 The air pollution **drifts** into the clouds. What does the word "drifts" mean?

- ○ floats
- ○ sails
- ○ flies
- ○ falls

3 If you wanted to find out more causes of air pollution and acid rain, which resource would be the most helpful?

- ○ dictionary
- ○ atlas
- ○ encyclopedia
- ○ thesaurus

4 Which word best completes the following sentence?

The factory owners are concerned about acid rain.

_____ doing the best they can to reduce the amount of air pollution they create.

- ○ Their
- ○ There
- ○ They're
- ○ They's

5 Look at the list Keisha made to teach her class about air pollution.

Sources of Air Pollution

1. Factories   3. Bikes
2. Cars   4. Buses

Which item does not belong on her list?

- ○ cars
- ○ bikes
- ○ buses
- ○ factories

6 Which word would finish this analogy?

Falling is to **getting hurt** like **air pollution** is to _____.

- ○ overcrowding
- ○ fog
- ○ acid rain
- ○ wind

Integrating Science with Reading Instruction · 3–4 © 2002 Creative Teaching Press

Name _____ Date _____

Get Logical

Marilyn, LaDawn, Sidney, and Keisha do things every week that are related to reducing air pollution and acid rain. Use the clues below to decide what each person does.

Clues

1 Sidney gets a lot of exercise while getting around town and helps to reduce acid rain at the same time.

2 Marilyn separates plastic throwaway items from paper throwaway items.

3 LaDawn's way of getting to work is better for the environment than her friend Scott's. He drives a car that gives off a lot of exhaust!

4 Keisha likes to save electricity in her home.

	Marilyn	LaDawn	Sidney	Keisha
Recycles				
Turns off the lights when not using them				
Rides a bike to the store				
Drives an electric car				

Marilyn _____.

LaDawn _____.

Sidney _____.

Keisha _____.

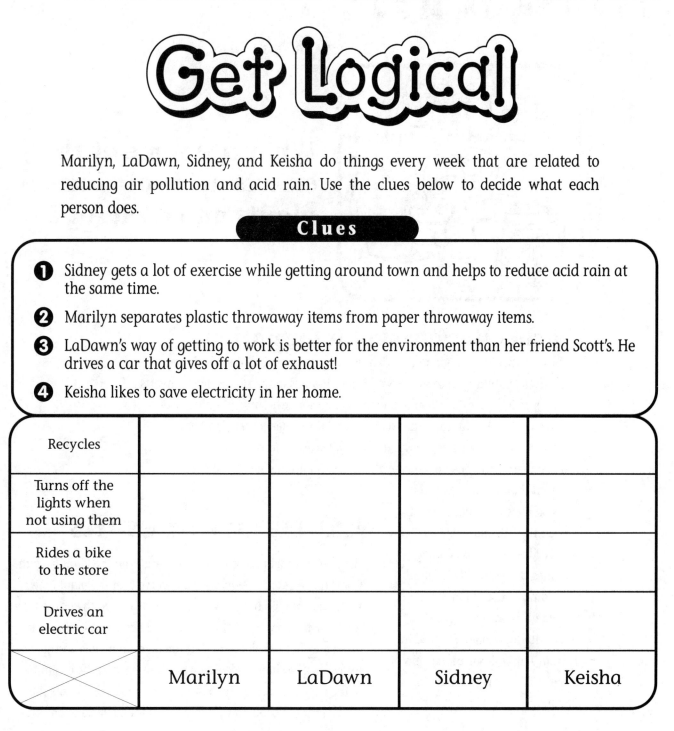

Acid Rain

What are some of the effects acid rain has on plants and buildings?

Teacher Background Information

Acid rain forms in the atmosphere when waste gases from burning fossil fuels (e.g., coal, oil, natural gas) combine with water droplets in the clouds. This converts the water to a weak acid. When the acid rain falls to the ground, it is absorbed into the soil. Plants with roots that soak up acid rainwater can be damaged in many ways. These plants may have discolored leaves or damaged roots. They may also lose their leaves or stop growing altogether. Eventually, it can kill the plants.

Acid rain that falls in lakes and rivers pollutes the water there and impacts the fish and wildlife in the area. Acid rain can also damage buildings. It is especially harmful to buildings made of limestone, marble, and concrete (which is made with limestone). The acid in the rain slowly dissolves the lime in the rock, causing the buildings to crumble bit by bit.

Experiment Results

Have each student record his or her results on the Plant Growth Chart (page 132). Students should observe that the plant grown with acid rain did not grow as tall or look as healthy as the plant grown with tap water. They will most likely notice that the leaves are somewhat discolored or that the plant may have lost some of its leaves. The chalk appeared white and hard at the beginning of the experiment. After exposure to the vinegar, students should notice that the chalk started fizzing or making little bubbles. The next day, the chalk will most likely be very soft or have completely fallen apart. The rock will also feel hard at the beginning of the experiment. Students will notice some small bubbles rising from the surface of the rock when it is placed in the vinegar. The next day, the rock will not look much different and it will still feel hard. It takes a long time for acid rain to completely destroy a rock.

Integrating Science with Reading Instruction · 3–4 © 2002 Creative Teaching Press

Acid Rain

What are some of the effects acid rain has on plants and buildings?

Procedure

1 Mix 1 tablespoon (15 mL) of vinegar in a pitcher of water. (Be careful not to spill the vinegar and keep it away from your eyes.) This mixture will represent your "acid rain." Prepare additional amounts as needed. (This experiment will last approximately 2 weeks.)

2 Place both potted plants in a sunny location. Water one plant with regular tap water. (This is your control plant. You will use it for a comparison.)

3 Water the second plant with the acid rain water you prepared.

4 Water both plants the same amount as needed for the next two weeks (about once every other day). Observe their growth every day for ten days.

5 Record your results on your Plant Growth Chart.

6 Observe and feel the chalk and the rock sample. Notice how hard or soft they are. Place a piece of chalk in a small paper cup. Place your rock sample in another cup. Cover the chalk and rock sample with vinegar. Observe what happens.

7 Wait one day and observe the items again. Remove the chalk and rock from the vinegar. Notice what they look like. Feel the chalk and the rock to observe any changes in hardness.

MATERIALS

(per group)
- ✔ Plant Growth Chart (page 132)
- ✔ measuring spoons
- ✔ vinegar
- ✔ 2 pitchers of water
- ✔ 2 small potted plants (flower or vegetable)
- ✔ pieces of chalk
- ✔ rock sample (limestone, concrete, or marble)
- ✔ 2 small paper cups

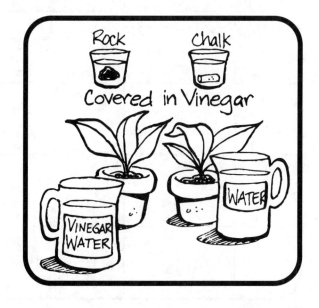

Integrating Science with Reading Instruction · 3–4 © 2002 Creative Teaching Press

Name _____   Date _____

 # Plant Growth Chart

Date	Height of Control Plant	Description of Control Plant	Height of Acid Rain Plant	Description of Acid Rain Plant

Integrating Science with Reading Instruction · 3–4 © 2002 Creative Teaching Press

Name _____   Date _____

Acid Rain

What are some of the effects acid rain has on plants and buildings?

Results and Conclusions

1 What were the main effects "acid rain" had on your plant?

_____

2 How did the chalk appear at the beginning of the experiment?

_____

3 How hard did the chalk feel?

_____

4 What happened when you poured vinegar (a weak acid) over the chalk?

_____

5 How did the chalk look and feel the next day?

_____

6 How did your rock sample appear at the beginning of the experiment?

_____

7 How hard did your rock sample feel?

_____

8 What happened when you poured vinegar (a weak acid) over the rock?

_____

9 How did the rock look and feel the next day?

_____

10 What are some of the effects acid rain has on plants and buildings?

_____

Integrating Science with Reading Instruction · 3–4 © 2002 Creative Teaching Press

Catch a Clue

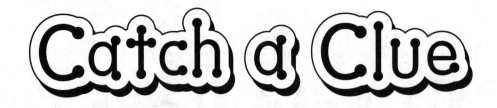

What will we learn about in our reading today?

electricity

solar system

storm

weather

Our Clues

❶ It was discovered.

❷ Your life would be very difficult without it.

❸ It can be weak or strong.

❹ It is in your car, your house, and your classroom.

Concept Map

Facts we already know about **electricity,** and the new facts we have learned

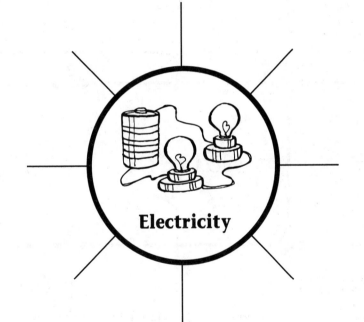

Electricity

Word Warm-Up

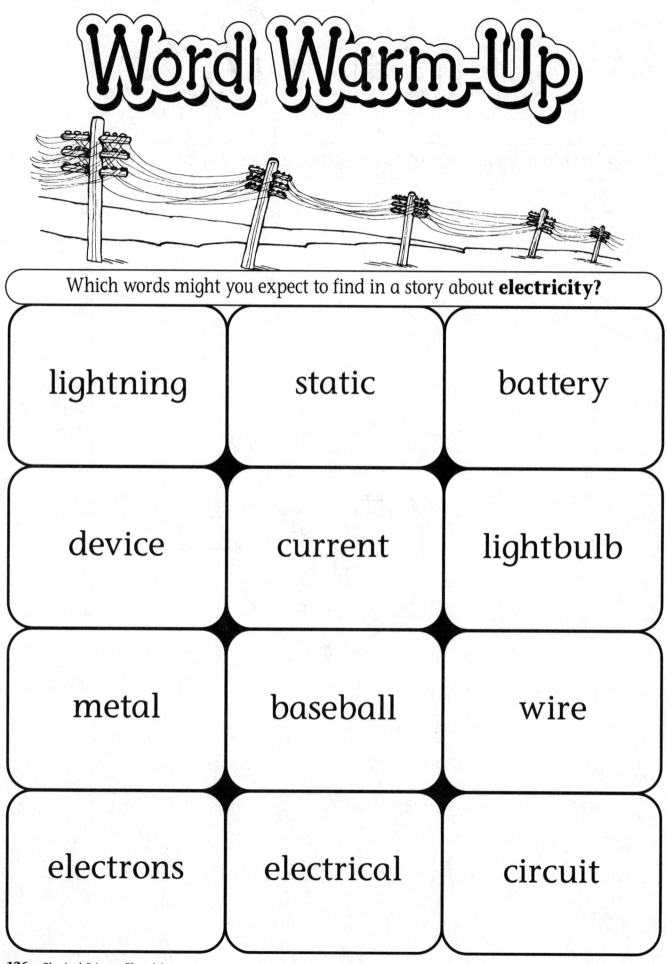

Which words might you expect to find in a story about **electricity?**

lightning	static	battery
device	current	lightbulb
metal	baseball	wire
electrons	electrical	circuit

Integrating Science with Reading Instruction · 3–4 © 2002 Creative Teaching Press

Electricity

When you use your lights, computer, and toaster, what are you using? Electricity! When you see lightning in the sky, what are you looking at? Electricity! When you rub a balloon on top of your head, what are you creating? Electricity! Electricity is everywhere. What is electricity? It is energy that we use each day but cannot see. Ben Franklin discovered the strong electrical jolt made by lightning when he flew a kite in a storm.

Lightning is a strong form of one type of electricity. It is called static electricity. This is a set of electrical charges that build up on an object. Static electricity is something you can create yourself! Slide your feet across the carpet in your socks. Then, touch a friend. When you do this, your socks pick up electrons. Electrons cause you and your friend to feel a shock.

Static electricity has two kinds of charges. One is negative. One is positive. If an object with a negative charge is near an object with a positive charge, they will stick to each other. This is what makes static cling in your clothes. But, when the same charges face each other, they push each other away. Static electricity happens when the weather is dry and cold.

Another kind of electricity is called current electricity. It flows in a loop, or circuit. There are many kinds of circuits. A simple circuit has one type of device (e.g., lightbulb, motor) in its loop that uses electricity. If the flow is broken, the electricity will stop. A simple circuit has a battery. It also has a device and wires to hold its parts (e.g., wire, lightbulb, battery) together. A simple circuit may have a switch to start and stop it.

Integrating Science with Reading Instruction · 3–4 © 2002 Creative Teaching Press

A series circuit has more than one device in the loop. These types of circuits are like playing baseball. You start at home plate and have to touch all the bases before you can reach home plate again. In a series circuit, the electricity must flow through every part in the circuit before it can go back to the battery.

Batteries are a common source of electricity. All batteries are not the same. Some are able to move electricity with more force. The more voltage a battery has, the more it is able to push electricity through a circuit. Have you ever put batteries in a game or radio? Watch carefully the next time you do. You will see metal bumps at the top of the battery that will touch other metal parts in the game or radio to complete the circuit.

It is easy to make your own circuit! All you need is one or two D batteries, some wire, and a flashlight bulb. Use the wire to hook the battery to the lightbulb in a circle. The lightbulb will shine when the loop is complete. If you remove the wire or the battery, then the circuit is broken and the light will go out. Have fun testing electricity, but always be careful and have an adult help you!

Integrating Science with Reading Instruction · 3–4 © 2002 Creative Teaching Press

Comprehension Questions

Literal Questions

1. What are the two kinds of electricity?

2. Who first discovered electricity?

3. How can you make a circuit?

4. How can you make static electricity?

5. What type of circuit has only one type of device in it?

Inferential Questions

1. Why is there a rubber covering around the cord of an electrical appliance?

2. What would happen if all of the electricity went out in your neighborhood?

3. What type of electricity are you creating when you rub a balloon on your head?

4. Why do parents of small children often put plastic plug covers in the sockets of their homes?

5. Have you ever gotten a shock? When is this most likely to occur?

Making Connections

1. What kinds of electricity have you used today?

2. Make a list of five safety rules you should follow when dealing with electrical appliances or experimenting with electricity.

3. Design a circuit. What kind of circuit is it? How would it be used?

4. How is electricity wasted? What can we do to conserve it?

Sharpen Your Skills

Name _____   **Date** _____

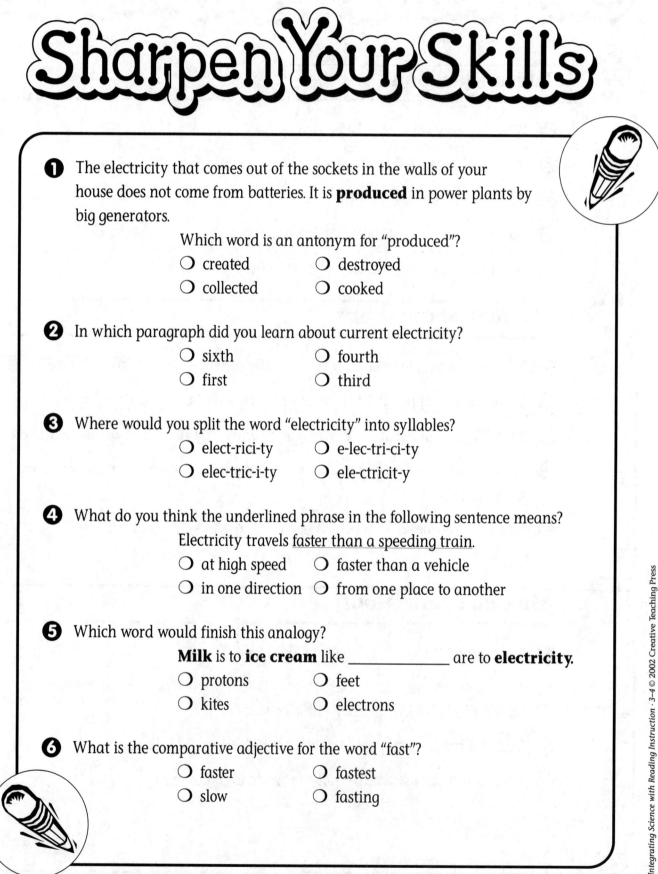

1 The electricity that comes out of the sockets in the walls of your house does not come from batteries. It is **produced** in power plants by big generators.

Which word is an antonym for "produced"?
- ○ created
- ○ collected
- ○ destroyed
- ○ cooked

2 In which paragraph did you learn about current electricity?
- ○ sixth
- ○ first
- ○ fourth
- ○ third

3 Where would you split the word "electricity" into syllables?
- ○ elect-rici-ty
- ○ elec-tric-i-ty
- ○ e-lec-tri-ci-ty
- ○ ele-ctricit-y

4 What do you think the underlined phrase in the following sentence means?
Electricity travels <u>faster than a speeding train</u>.
- ○ at high speed
- ○ in one direction
- ○ faster than a vehicle
- ○ from one place to another

5 Which word would finish this analogy?
Milk is to **ice cream** like _____ are to **electricity**.
- ○ protons
- ○ kites
- ○ feet
- ○ electrons

6 What is the comparative adjective for the word "fast"?
- ○ faster
- ○ slow
- ○ fastest
- ○ fasting

Integrating Science with Reading Instruction · 3–4 © 2002 Creative Teaching Press

The Science Club at Weaver Elementary School decided to do some experiments related to electricity. The club was divided into four groups. Before they could begin, each group needed to learn about one specific topic. Use the clues below to decide what topic each group chose.

Clues

1 Group 2 chose to learn about how electricity travels in a circle.

2 Group 4 wanted to learn about collecting electrons, shocking their friends, and making their hair stand up straight.

3 Group 1 wanted to learn about the source of electricity used in their portable radios and flashlights.

4 The third group read more about measuring the force that pushes the electric current along.

	Group 1	Group 2	Group 3	Group 4
Voltage				
Batteries				
Circuits				
Static Electricity				

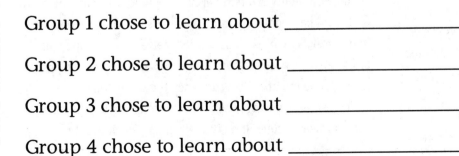

Group 1 chose to learn about _____.

Group 2 chose to learn about _____.

Group 3 chose to learn about _____.

Group 4 chose to learn about _____.

Integrating Science with Reading Instruction · 3–4 © 2002 Creative Teaching Press

Electricity

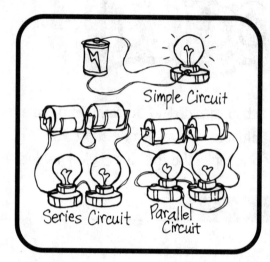

Simple Circuit

Series Circuit

Parallel Circuit

What is the difference between simple, series, and parallel electric circuits?

Teacher Background Information

Electric circuits provide a path for the electricity to flow from the battery through all of the devices and then return to the battery. A simple circuit only has one light. That lightbulb will look bright because it can receive all the electricity it needs. In a series circuit, the electric current flows through each device, one after the other, when the circuit is complete. Lights connected in a series will not be as bright because they have to share the electricity that is flowing. In addition, all of the electricity available must flow through each light as it goes along. This creates more resistance, and results in less electricity flowing in the circuit. The brightness of the lights depends on how much electricity each bulb receives. If one light in a series circuit goes out, or you unscrew one lightbulb, the circuit is broken and all of the lights go out. In a series circuit, either everything is on or everything is off. When devices are wired in a parallel circuit, the electric current flows in more than one path. Each device has its own supply of electricity. If you unscrew one light in a parallel circuit while the current is on, the other light(s) will stay on because each light has its own supply of electricity. The insulated bell wire should be 20–22 gauge, the flashlight bulbs should be 1.5–3 volts, and the porcelain or plastic light sockets can be purchased from a hardware store.

Experiment Results

In the simple circuit, the lightbulb should appear bright. In the series circuit with two bulbs, both of the bulbs will appear dim because they must share the electricity between them. When students unscrew one lightbulb in the series circuit, the other light will also go out. This happens because the circuit is broken and the electricity cannot get back to the battery to complete the circuit. Both lights in a parallel circuit will look bright. These two bulbs will be brighter than the two bulbs wired in a series circuit. In a parallel circuit, each lightbulb receives its own supply of electricity and does not have to wait for the electricity to pass through one bulb before it can reach the second one. When students unscrew one lightbulb in a parallel circuit, the other light stays on because it has its own supply of electricity.

Integrating Science with Reading Instruction · 3–4 © 2002 Creative Teaching Press

Electricity

What is the difference between simple, series, and parallel electric circuits?

Procedure

1 Use the wire stripper to remove the insulation from the ends of each piece of wire.

2 Insert the two D batteries into the holder. Notice that they fit in opposite directions. One end with the bump will be at the top of the holder, and the other bump end will be at the bottom.

3 Screw each flashlight bulb into a small socket. (Use the screwdriver to connect the wires to the light socket.)

4 Use two wires, the batteries, and one flashlight bulb to create a simple circuit. Notice how bright or dim the light is when you complete the circuit.

5 Use three wires, two flashlight bulbs, and the batteries to create a series circuit. Then, unscrew one bulb while the current is on and observe what happens.

6 Use four wires, two flashlight bulbs, and the batteries to create a parallel circuit. In a parallel circuit, each light will have its own path of electricity. Notice how bright or dim the lights are. Then, unscrew one lightbulb and observe what happens.

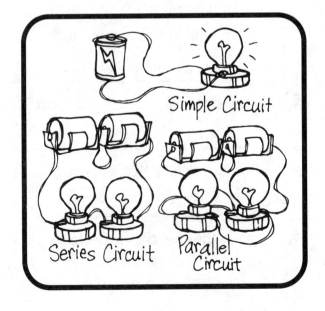

Simple Circuit

Series Circuit

Parallel Circuit

Name _____   Date _____

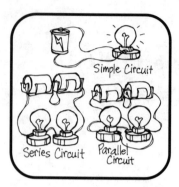

Simple Circuit

Series Circuit   Parallel Circuit

Electricity

What is the difference between simple, series, and parallel electric circuits?

Results and Conclusions

1 How do you know your circuits were complete?

_____

2 In your simple circuit, was the lightbulb bright or dim?

_____

3 In your series circuit, were the lightbulbs bright or dim?

_____

4 In your parallel circuit, were the lightbulbs bright or dim?

_____

5 What happened in your series circuit when you unscrewed one lightbulb?

_____

Why do you think this happened?

_____

6 What happened in your parallel circuit when you unscrewed one lightbulb?

_____

Why do you think this happened?

_____

7 What is the difference between simple, series, and parallel electric circuits?

_____

Integrating Science with Reading Instruction · 3–4 © 2002 Creative Teaching Press

Answer Key

Page 9

ocean communities

Page 11

coral, sea anemones, barnacles, animals, zones, murky, twilight

Page 14

Literal Questions
1. body of salt water
2. Sunlight Zone, Twilight Zone, and Midnight Zone
3. clams, mole crabs, worms, and sand dollars
4. sea urchins, sea anemones, sea stars, hermit crabs, barnacles, mussels, limpets, and chiton
5. the sea level falls

Inferential Questions
Answers will vary. Accept all reasonable responses.

Making Connections
Answers will vary. Accept all reasonable responses.

Page 15

1. collect–conjunction
2. die
3. encyclopedia
4. ocean
5. barnacles
6. dive

Page 16

Reggie–Midnight Zone
Shasta–Sandy Beach
Carmine–Coral Reef
Shirley–Tide Pools

Page 19

Answers will vary. Possible answers include:
1. low spots or depressions
2. high tide
3. snail
4. sea star and crab
5. crab
6. low tide
7. The tide pool is found along a rocky shore.
8. Some animals close up and store water inside their shells. Others move to deeper waters or find a pool to stay in until the high tide returns.

Page 20

our skeleton

Page 22

pivot, protects, guard, organs, tendons, hinge, socket, gliding, tissue

Page 25

Literal Questions
1. 206 bones; 26 bones
2. strong stretchy bands that connect bones together
3. vertebrae
4. ball-and-socket, hinge, pivot, gliding, immovable, and partially movable
5. bones will weaken

Inferential Questions
Answers will vary. Accept all reasonable responses.

Making Connections
Answers will vary. Accept all reasonable responses.

Page 26

1. fraction–fragile
2. protect
3. 128
4. joints
5. smooth
6. bones

Page 27

James–Tendons
Marcus–Joints
Tarek–Ligaments
Gwen–Muscles

Page 30

Answers will vary. Accept all reasonable responses.

Page 31

Answers will vary. Possible answers include:
1. round column
2. round; helps the bone to distribute weight evenly
3. hard and smooth
4. bone marrow; soft and spongy instead of hard and smooth
5. strong–shape and flexibility; lightweight–center is filled with marrow
6. shape and flexibility of the bones

Page 32

food chains

Page 34

nutrients, energy, healthy, plankton, survive, carbon dioxide, garbage decomposer, consumer

Page 37

Literal Questions
1. shows how living things eat other living things to survive
2. producer, consumer, and decomposer
3. carnivore–eats meat; herbivore–eats plants; omnivore–eats plants and animals
4. Sun provides energy to help producers create their own food.
5. consumers; producers

Inferential Questions
Answers will vary. Accept all reasonable responses.

Making Connections
Answers will vary. Accept all reasonable responses.

Page 38

1. preserved
2. encyclopedia
3. takes
4. producer
5. and
6. om-ni-vore

Page 39

Shanelle–Carnivores
Colby–Herbivores
Calvin–Producers
Elton–Decomposers

Page 43

Answers will vary. Possible answers include:
1. The sun and rain clouds supply natural energy to the producers.
2. grasshopper
3. Yes; Yes; The number of consumers varies from one environment to another.
4. No; Without producers, some consumers would not have anything to eat.
5. garbage dump
6. omnivore or herbivore
7. It shows the natural order of consumption.

Page 44

rain forests

Page 46

tropical, understory, layers, medicine, endangered, shady, cashew nut, emergent, species

Page 49

Literal Questions
1. cutting down or clearing of trees
2. It destroys plant and animal habitats.
3. forest floor, understory, canopy layer, and emergent layer
4. canopy layer
5. bananas, pineapples, coconuts, and cashew nuts

Inferential Questions
Answers will vary. Accept all reasonable responses.

Making Connections
Answers will vary. Accept all reasonable responses.

Page 50

1. five
2. encyclopedia
3. bed
4. Tropical rain forests are close to the equator.
5. bottom
6. their

Page 51

Marcus–Emergent Layer
Pierre–Canopy Layer
Mary–Forest Floor
Penelope–Understory

Page 54

Answers will vary. Possible answers include:
1. Temperatures will vary depending upon the time of day and year.
2. almost all
3. very little
4. The temperature increased by a few degrees.
5. The temperature changed very little, if any at all.
6. The temperature would stay fairly constant during the day.
7. No; Each layer has different living environments and food resources.
8. emergent layer and canopy layer
9. understory and forest floor
10. The rain forest provides a large variety of living environments.

Page 55

earthquakes

Page 57

movement, tremble, force, layers, fault, pressure, vibration, Richter scale

Page 60

Literal Questions
1. a sudden movement in the earth's crust
2. when rock layers break because of too much pressure on them
3. stand in a doorway, get under a desk, and stay away from windows
4. seismograph
5. Richter scale

Inferential Questions
Answers will vary. Accept all reasonable responses.

Making Connections
Answers will vary. Accept all reasonable responses.

Page 61

1. to write
2. severe
3. atlas
4. d
5. vibrations
6. earth-quake

Page 62

Jennifer–7.0
Brenton–4.5
Linda–3.0
Richard–2.0

Page 65

Answers will vary. Possible answers include:
1. moved sideways, sliding past each other; shear
2. trees and houses fell over, small crack developed in the soil surface
3. some fell over
4. where the pieces of material meet; more movement occurred here
5. The sudden movement of the earth's crustal plates cause earthquakes. In an earthquake the plates can be pulled apart (tension), be pushed together (compression), or slide past each other (shear).

Page 66

volcanoes

Page 68

magma, erupt, blowhole, shield, destroys, Hawaii, extinct, activity, pumice, explode

Page 71

Literal Questions
1. shield volcano, composite volcano, and cinder cone volcano
2. cinder cone volcano
3. shield volcano and composite volcano
4. shield volcano
5. magma (melted rock) that erupts out of volcanoes; Lava changes form by cooling down.

Inferential Questions
Answers will vary. Accept all reasonable responses.

Making Connections
Answers will vary. Accept all reasonable responses.

Page 72

1. crater
2. dictionary
3. Composite volcanoes shoot lava through the air when they erupt.
4. homophones
5. hot
6. vol-ca-nic

Page 73

Jonah–Cinder Cone Volcano
Rosie–Shield Volcano
Lorraine–Composite Volcano

Page 76

Answers will vary. Accept all reasonable responses.

Page 77

Answers will vary. Possible answers include:
1. alike–feel hard, all the rocks are shades of dark or drab colors; different–surface texture
2. Accept all reasonable responses.
3. Accept all reasonable responses.
4. Accept all reasonable responses.
5. Magma originates from different locations in each volcano causing the magma to cool at different speeds.

Page 78

water pollution

Page 80

natural resource, wastewater, agriculture, chemicals, trash can, recycled, pollute, drink, animals, poison

Page 83

Literal Questions
1. wastewater, oil spill, chemical
2. Throw trash in a trashcan.
3. A place where wastewater is cleaned with special chemicals then released.
4. The trash pollutes rivers and oceans.
5. Reused water is used to water golf courses and parks.

Inferential Questions
Answers will vary. Accept all reasonable responses.

Making Connections
Answers will vary. Accept all reasonable responses.

Page 84
1. contact–contradict
2. contaminate
3. encyclopedia
4. Justin took it for granted that the river water was safe to drink.
5. oil spill
6. their

Page 85
Paul–Sorts trash for recycling
Marla–Takes a shorter shower
Carlotta–Turns off the water while brushing teeth
Trenton–Washes full loads of laundry

Page 88
Answers will vary. Possible answers include:
1. No; "Agricultural chemicals" are dissolved in the water and chemical pieces are not visible.
2. Yes; Pollution is visible.
3. Yes; Pollution is visible.
4. street trash
5. agricultural chemicals
6. By just looking at the water it would not be obvious that the water is polluted.
7. Accept all reasonable responses.

Page 89
our solar system

Page 91
All words should be chosen.

Page 94
Literal Questions
1. Mercury, Venus, Earth, Mars, Jupiter, Saturn, Uranus, Neptune
2. eight planets, the Sun, dwarf planets, many moons, and other space objects.
3. Saturn
4. Mars
5. telescope at night

Inferential Questions
Answers will vary. Accept all reasonable responses.

Making Connections
Answers will vary. Accept all reasonable responses.

Page 95
1. orator–orchid
2. thesaurus
3. Pluto
4. There is a band of the color red in each rainbow.
5. through
6. spin

Page 96
Hector–Mercury
Summer–Pluto
Sharon–Mars
Shana–Saturn

Page 99
Answers will vary. Possible answers include:
1. tired; hard; The book seemed to become heavier as time went by.
2. No; Gravity pulled the tennis ball to the floor.
3. inertia
4. gravity; down
5. The eraser flies away; away from me
6. pulled on the string
7. gravity and inertia

Page 100
sound energy

Page 102

All words should be chosen.

Page 105

Literal Questions

1. people talking, music, traffic, and alarm clocks
2. solids
3. striking, stroking, plucking, and blowing
4. Sound is produced because an object moves back and forth quickly.
5. Sound waves press together and then separate moving from where the wave began to the waves destination.

Inferential Questions

Answers will vary. Accept all reasonable responses.

Making Connections

Answers will vary. Accept all reasonable responses.

Page 106

1. heating
2. decided
3. thesaurus
4. stroking
5. plucking
6. loudest

Page 107

Jackson-Sand Blocks
Eli-Flute
Jasmine-Guitar
Dana-Drums

Page 110

Answers will vary. Possible answers include:

1. craft sticks, comb, bell, and straw
2. craft sticks and straws
3. comb and rubber band
4. straws
5. violin; Waves vibrate faster in the smaller body of the violin.
6. by varying how fast an object vibrates

Page 111

light energy

Page 113

retina, roller coaster, angle, waves, colors, energy, refraction, reflection, lasers

Page 116

Literal Questions

1. form of energy; waves; 186,000 miles (300,000 km) per second
2. make lasers, holograms, photographs, and medicine
3. bending of light
4. light bouncing off of an object
5. changes into heat

Inferential Questions

Answers will vary. Accept all reasonable responses.

Making Connections

Answers will vary. Accept all reasonable responses.

Page 117

1. realize-related
2. take in
3. title page
4. reflect
5. black outside and black interior
6. clear

Page 118

Chloe-Reflection
Linda-Light Is Made of Many Colors
Monica-Refraction
Erik-Changing Light into Heat Energy

Page 121

Answers will vary. Possible answers include:
1. the overhead transparency
2. the overhead transparency; has the smoothest surface
3. yes
4. number will vary; by holding the mirrors parallel; light is being reflected back and forth repeatedly
5. The penny appeared to have moved.
6. refracted
7. Reflected light bounces back and refracted light bends.

Page 122

acid rain

Page 124

harmful, toxic, pollution, gasoline, vehicles, waste, gases, asthma, marble, children

Page 127

Literal Questions
1. air pollution
2. The air pollutants combine with water droplets in the clouds to form acid which then falls as acid rain.
3. asthma, coughing, headaches, and scratchy throats
4. When plants absorb acid rain they can become dangerous for animals or people to eat or the plants could die.
5. crowded cities; more air pollution is produced

Inferential Questions
Answers will vary. Accept all reasonable responses.

Making Connections
Answers will vary. Accept all reasonable responses.

Page 128

1. metal
2. floats
3. encyclopedia
4. They're
5. bikes
6. acid rain

Page 129

Marilyn-Recycles
LaDawn-Drives an electric car
Sidney-Rides a bike to the store
Keisha-Turns off the lights when not using them

Page 132

Answers will vary. Accept all reasonable responses.

Page 133

Answers will vary. Possible answers include:
1. plant didn't grow as tall and looked unhealthy
2. looked like a normal piece of chalk
3. like a pretzel stick
4. The chalk started to fizz.
5. soft or completely fallen apart
6. looked like a normal rock
7. very hard
8. Small bubbles rose from the rock's surface.
9. The rock looked and felt the same.
10. Acid rain creates unhealthy plants and can slowly deteriorate buildings.

Page 134

electricity

Page 136

All words should be chosen.

Page 137

Literal Questions

1. static electricity and current electricity
2. Ben Franklin
3. connect a wire to a battery and then to a light bulb
4. rubbing a balloon on top of your head
5. simple circuit

Inferential Questions

Answers will vary. Accept all reasonable responses.

Making Connections

Answers will vary. Accept all reasonable responses.

Page 140

1. destroyed
2. fourth
3. elec-tric-i-ty
4. at high speed
5. electrons
6. faster

Page 141

Group 1–Batteries
Group 2–Circuits
Group 3–Voltage
Group 4–Static Electricity

Page 144

Answers will vary. Possible answers include:

1. the lightbulbs turned on
2. bright
3. dim
4. bright
5. the other light went out; circuit is broken
6. the other light stays on; circuit is not broken
7. A simple circuit has one device. A series circuit has two devices which electricity has to pass through. In a parallel circuit the current flows in more than one path.